# From Happiness to Tragedy; to Bliss on the Borderline

# From Happiness to Tragedy; to Bliss on the Borderline

## (Lamentations of a Fool)

Nicholas E. Cleveland

Proverbs 19
Proverbs 31:10–31

*AuthorHouse™*
*1663 Liberty Drive*
*Bloomington, IN 47403*
*www.authorhouse.com*
*Phone: 1 (800) 839-8640*



*Published by AuthorHouse 2/03/2015*

*ISBN: 978-1-4969-6636-0 (sc)*
*ISBN: 978-1-4969-6637-7 (e)*

*Library of Congress Control Number: 2015901691*

# Contents

## Part II: She Left Me Again



## Part III: My Second Love

## Part IV: On the Borderline



## Part V: Afterthought after the Afterthought

*To those who have experienced bliss*
*only to have it*
*turn into pain and misery.*

# Introduction

Bewildered, she exclaimed, "Did she have psychological problems?"

I was stunned. I had just told my real estate agent that I was selling my house because my wife had left me nine months earlier.

A few years ago, we'd bought a house in the Akron area. My wife rode around town with this real estate agent looking for a home. When I told the agent she had left me, she said, "She talked you up so well. I honestly believed she thought you were a god!"

I replied, "I used to be, but now I'm a demon from Hades." Neither my wife nor I had spoken to this agent since she'd sold us our house.

That's just a small sample of the paradox I had lived the previous twelve years. My first wife died suddenly, leaving me alone with our seven-year-old boy. A year later, I married my second wife. Now, my second period of grieving was to begin.

Through the course of the following pages, you will cruise along the path of a man who laments the loss of his first wife and tries to make sense of life in general. Suddenly, however, in the midst of the book (Part II), his second wife leaves him. This devastation twists the book into a peculiar direction as he expresses his grief in the loss of her, his second wife. Then, in part three, he tells his story of the agonies involved in living with this woman (second wife) whom he realizes has borderline personality disorder. In part four, the book produces evidence that convinces him she has borderline personality disorder and then elaborates further on how it affected him and his son. Finally, in part five, as an afterthought, he discusses the fact that he may be narcissistic after all and this narcissism may have drawn him to his BPD wife and helps explain how they stayed together for so long.

# Author's Note

So the reader better understands the flow of the following pages, I must explain the sudden changes in tense from past to present and back to past again. As I reflected upon my life, I thought it good to put to paper my understanding of why I had experienced the things I had over the past 59 years. As I pondered these things, trying to make sense of them all, I mixed in tidbits of my own wisdom, if it can be called such. Nonetheless, my understanding of the way things are and the way things should be are in much conflict.

My major and most horrifying experience starts the book out. It occurred years ago. I then pen the way things were, during better days. Then I go off on a moral tangent, then flashback again. At times, I reminisce the way things presently are, while penning the pages below. This is the confusing part that needs explanation.

Whenever you read present tense, it is my experience, right then and there, while writing this book. I write my thoughts as they happen, then flashback to a day in the past, then flip to my philosophical understanding of life, and back again. I sincerely hope you can follow; but this is my life: Confusing, complicated, trying, yet wonderful.

Please enjoy the ride.
Nicholas E Cleveland

# PART I

# My First Love

# A Rude Slumber

"Honey. Honey! *Honey!*"

I shook her.

She was cold.

I looked at her face, *not* expecting the worse. She was still as death. I felt her arm. It was cold. Her skin had begun to turn blue. It was clammy.

Just a couple of months earlier, on Thanksgiving weekend, my wife and I experienced the worse argument we had ever had in our lives. The holidays went fine. They were the usual. My wife and I, along with our seven-year-old son, went to her family's home for our first of two heavy holiday meals.

My mother-in-law was a traditional, down-home southern lady. She believed her mission in life was to overstuff her family with good food. She succeeded. I recall my first holiday meal there. It was an experience for wide eyes and a large stomach. I don't recall the number of courses, but there must have been a dozen. Ham, turkey, mashed potatoes, sweet potatoes, scalloped potatoes, corn, green beans (the beans always had large pieces of bacon), baked beans (with large strips of bacon), cranberry sauce (the kind that still looks like the can when it is served), home-baked bread, home-baked dinner rolls, butter, apple butter, honey, jelly, and other foods I don't presently recall. For dessert, it was usually the same thing every holiday. We had the best homemade apple pie made from scratch and the freshest apples this side of the Pacific, cherry pie, cherry cheesecake, chocolate pie, and banana pudding. As for drinks, we had milk, cranberry-apple juice, and strong coffee.

I had learned to strengthen my coffee from two level scoops per pot when I was a young man to seven heaping scoops per pot. To this day, I use seven scoops. After all, seven is the perfect number,[1] and the Bible named a book[2] after this ritual. Shortly after I had finished that home-cooked southern feast, I sat on the couch, staring at the wall for the rest of the afternoon. I couldn't move. I believe it was the first time I had experienced such a swelling sensation in my stomach that froze me in my tracks. First of all, I couldn't believe I'd eaten that much, and second, I couldn't stop thinking, *Oh no, am I going to explode?*

For the second part of the holiday, we visited my parents. My mom and dad were more traditional in the sense I understood it. They were from the northern part of the country—Michigan. My dad's parents came from French-speaking Canada around the turn of the twentieth century. They were farmers who believed in birthing farmhands in addition to hiring them. Dad had eleven brothers and sisters of which he was the youngest. I recall as a youngster visiting my cousins and hearing them call my dad Uncle. Dad was younger than they were, and it took me some time to realize that a grandmother could have a child after her son had one. He had a few nieces and nephews who were older than him.

Anyway, his parents were very old by the time I came along. I fondly recall as a child how the family would climb into our 1959 Chevy—Mom, Dad, and six kids (baby on Mom's lap, second youngest in the middle, and the rest of us in the backseat). We'd travel an hour and a half to the hilly country of Hillsdale, Michigan. I was mesmerized by the mountains on the way there (actually, they were small hills, but I lived in the flatlands west of Lake Erie and south of the mouth of the Detroit River). Finally, after what seemed like a large portion of my young lifetime, we turned down a gravel road. After traveling it for approximately a mile, we'd spot the green-shingled farmhouse. Everyone in the backseat would shout at the same time, "We're here!"

The long driveway led up to a barn, and before we could get out of the car, Grandpa and Grandma would run from the porch exclaiming, "They're here!" Before we knew it, they were hugging and kissing each of us as we entered the old farmhouse.

Once in, Grandpa would say to my dad, "I told your mom you'd be out today."

In the kitchen was a manual-pump faucet on the edge of the sink, a large dining table, and a wood cooking stove alongside a gas stove. My dad had purchased the gas stove for Grandma, but she didn't want to get it dirty so she continued to cook on the wood stove for a very long time. The kitchen sink hand pump was attached to a well. Hanging on the wall was a drinking scoop (a cup with a long handle on it) and next to that was a white towel. It took me years to understand the wisdom of my grandfather when he told me I washed my hands on the towel instead of in the soap and water.

In the next room were two rocking chairs, a potbellied stove, and another large dining table with many chairs around it. This is where I would beat my grandpa in arm wrestling when we weren't enjoying a homemade chicken-and-dumpling dinner. Speaking of dinner, let's get back to my parents for the remainder of the Thanksgiving holiday.

My dad cooked the turkey in a fryer outside. He purchased a gas fired fryer, which he filled with peanut oil, to burn the turkey in one year. We all decided, although very crispy, it tasted wonderful! Mom wasn't a southern cook, but her holiday meals were also great. Everyone brought a dish to pass, and my middle sister always made home-baked cream donuts. My favorite was peanut butter cream. Needless to say, by the time we made it to my parents on a holiday, my appetite was petite. The 254-course meal I had at my in-laws was just beginning to debloat. But I did force myself. Then after another good meal and good times, we headed back to the house.

# The Incident

It was two days later (the Saturday after Thanksgiving) when I told my wife I was going to clean the master bathroom. I was always one who liked a clean house. However, I believed it was the wife's job to do it. Not if she worked full time, necessarily, but if she worked part time, she had plenty of time to do housework. After all, I built the house. She should keep it clean!

I had gone back to college for approximately a year after taking a short ten-year break after high school. I was already tired of sitting in the classroom, so we purchased a wooded lot in a small farm community in southeastern Michigan. A couple of years after this purchase, I hired a contractor to dig a hole, and a mason and I installed the footing. After the basement block was laid, I built a conventional brick fireplace. A carpenter built the shell, but I installed the electrical, plumbing, heating, drywall, and wood trim. My wife and her dad installed the insulation.

Speaking of her dad, just a few months before we began construction on the house, he had experienced pain in his chest. During this episode, he drove himself twenty miles to the hospital. While in the ER, they told him he had just had a heart attack. He was immediately sent to intensive care.

He came out of it fine but was told he needed a multiple bypass. During the interim between his heart attack and his bypass surgery, he helped me build my house. My wife wouldn't let him do anything strenuous, but I didn't pay much attention as I was solely concerned with getting the house done. Whenever people came to help, I would crack the whip and get as much work out of them as possible.

I didn't realize till years later what an idiot I had been when people, out of the goodness of their hearts, came to lend me a hand. I was solely concerned with "getting it done." My life was one big get-it-done episode. Don't look at the cost to the individual. Just get it done!

This brings me to a lesson I have learned over the years. When I was younger, my sole vision in life was to pursue a goal. It didn't matter if I had fun pursuing it; I just needed to meet that goal. In my later years, I took a different approach. I began to enjoy the ride and not worry about pursuing goals or preparing for the future. That was also a mistake. I have presently found it is important to strike a balance. We must have goals and prepare for the future, but it is just as important to enjoy the pursuance of those goals and preparations. Certainly, we can't always do what we want and still gain the prize at the end. But, at the same time, we shouldn't be miserable all the time in trying to gain that prize. It's often the case anyway, when we reach our goals, that we find out they aren't quite as pretty or enjoyable as we thought they'd be. Sometimes it takes awhile for this reality to set in, but it always does. We need to set our destination *and* enjoy the ride on the way there.

Our house was about fifteen years old when my wife died, so some areas were in need of redecorating, things like wallpaper and paint. It had two and a half baths. The half bath was off the mudroom at the garage entrance. A full bath was between the living room and the bedrooms, just off the hall. The bathroom in question was the master bath.

When we built the house, we had no children. It was my wife's fault, we figured. She was the one who had polyglandular autoimmune syndrome. This is a disease where the antibodies in the blood think that the glands in your body aren't supposed to be there. As a result, they continuously attack the hormone-producing glands. These attacks, in turn, cause the glands not to produce or not to produce the proper quantity of hormones.

We found out about this disease a year or two before we built our house, which was also immediately after taking a two-week vacation in Michigan. Our travels began south of Detroit, then up the eastern coastline along Lake Huron and on to Mackinac. After visiting the island, we proceeded over the bridge on to the Soo Locks in Sault Ste. Marie. From there, we traveled west to many and various waterfalls. Some of the waterfalls were quite a hike into the woods. I noticed she didn't keep up with me as well as I would have liked, but I wrote it off to the fact that she was a girl. After visiting these waterfalls, Picture Rock, and the Iron Mountain iron mine, we headed back home. We traveled along Michigan's western coastline along Lake Michigan, through the Sleeping Bear sand dunes, and then the Silver Lake sand dunes. It was cherry season, so we always had sweet cherries to munch on that we purchased at the many roadside stands.

For dinner, we stopped at a restaurant on the water. The dock extended over the Lake Michigan shore, making a very nice dinner scene. Afterward, we drove south to Holland, Michigan. There we admired the beautiful tulips and the famous windmill in the middle of the miniature Dutch town. We then proceeded to cross Michigan eastward. We stopped at a few book manufacturers, including Baker Books and Erdmann's, for I had become quite the bookworm. In high school, however, I hated to read.

I embarrassingly recall my senior year English composition class, where I ignorantly selected the book *Dracula* to give a book report on. I had always enjoyed horror movies and figured I'd like this book, even though it was very thick. I soon found that reading horror was nowhere near as enjoyable as watching it. I recall standing at the front of the class giving my book report, but the only thing I really remember about the whole episode was the teacher asking me if I read the book. My answer was one of the most embarrassing moments of my young life when I replied, "Some of it." I got a D for dumb as a grade.

When my wife and I finally made it home, she began complaining of her extreme fatigue. After a day or two, it was so severe that I decided to take her to the clinic. The doctor told us she had the flu and just needed to rest. Two days later, when I came home from work, she was lying on the couch barely able to move. I told her we'd better get back to the clinic. She insisted she needed her hair washed before going outside the house, so as she lay on her back, I put her hair in a large pan and washed and dried it. She was so weak I had to carry her to the car and then into the clinic.

When the doctor saw her, he immediately sent her to the emergency room. They connected the IVs and began collaboration. It looked serious. They sent her to the

University of Michigan Hospital in Ann Arbor. For days, she laid there, barely able to move. The doctors still didn't have a diagnosis. There were continuous strings of medical professors and students parading in and out of her room. Finally, after approximately four days, a student doctor came into the room with an old book.

He said, "We finally know what is wrong with your wife. Here's a book on her disease."

I leafed through the book. There was a picture of a patient with my wife's disease lying in bed. A few days later, the patient looked worse and was extremely fatigued. As days went on, the patient grew worse and worse until finally he died. The book said they knew what caused the sickness but did not have the capability to cure it. In desperation, I looked up at the doctor, expecting him to explain why my wife was beginning to look better instead of worse.

He smiled and said, "This is an old book. We have since found a cure, and you're wife has nothing to worry about!"

I wanted to smack him down and then thank him, but as I was so happy they had a cure, I just thanked him. He told me the reason so many doctors had been in and out of the room was because they rarely saw a case like this. He said she had Polyglandular Autoimmune Syndrome, which is an expansion of Addison's disease. President John F. Kennedy had Addison's, and he was fine, medically, until that dreadful, unrelated, final day. Technology is now able to artificially produce cortisone, which is produced by the adrenalin gland (Addison's), and all other hormones produced by the glands. Hence, my wife had to take her hormones in pill form from that day forward.

As stated earlier, it was early in the morning on the Saturday after Thanksgiving when I told my wife I would clean the master bathroom. As I was the only one who used it (she had always used the main bath), she didn't think it was terrible that I would be the one to clean it (and now that I think about it, she was right). In addition, she had been feeling unusually weak for the past month or so. In the past few years, her arthritis had gradually gotten worse, but recently, it had appeared to be in remission. Nonetheless, she was very tired. So when she said she was tired, I thought, *So what? So am I!*

I commenced cleaning the bathroom. Just outside the door was a magazine rack full of magazines and catalogs. I saw no reason for these, so I picked them up and began walking out the back door. Suddenly, she appeared and stood in front of me.

She said, "What are you throwing away?"

After I told her they were just some old magazines, she quickly glanced through them and said she wanted to keep some of them. I told her it was too late; she had already had her chance. Then she made a wisecrack comment that made me so mad I said, "Get out of my way!"

She refused, so I grabbed the doorknob and opened the door, forcing her out of the way. I threw her magazines into the garbage can. I didn't think it was all that big of a deal, as they were junk as far as I was concerned. (Later, however, I realized some of them were historical magazines from our town, and she collected such paraphernalia). I soon forgot about the episode, but my wife didn't. A few weeks later, when she and I were talking in the kitchen, she said I should apologize to her for treating her the way I had that dreadful

Saturday after Thanksgiving. I told her if she ever blocked my way out of the house again, I would do the same thing! We had had arguments before, but nothing like that one. Still, I didn't apologize.

# It's Over

That Thanksgiving weekend argument will echo in my mind for eternity. My property taxes were due the following February 14th (*only 2 ½ months after the Thanksgiving incident and 5 days after my beloved 1st wife passed –approximately 13 years ago*). When paying them, the clerk asked, "Was that your wife I saw in the paper this week?" I confirmed that it had been. She said, "Well, I'm sure you have no regrets."

I just looked at her with a cold, hard stare and thought, *Lady, all I have is regrets.* Also, in those days, all I had was cold, hard stares.

I was in so much pain I didn't notice other people, their thoughts, or their feelings. I only had two constant thoughts. The first was, *Lord, please wake me up from this nightmare.* The second was, *I must be stable for the sake of my son.*

My pastor emeritus's wife gave me a magazine with an article in it by a famous coach who had lost his wife. In it, he told what he did to try and cope with his loss. I was already tired of people trying to console me, but at the same time, I needed for people to try and console me. The coach said there really was nothing that he did that allowed him to cope very well, but one thing did make him feel a little better. He walked. He also advised not to do anything stupid like selling the family home. I put it into my head that I would try to walk and not sell my house. I was successful, temporarily.

The walks seemed to clear the fogginess from my head a little bit. In the process, as I was also eating very little because my stomach was continuously upset from my torment, I lost fifty pounds in a period of ten months. I recall playing basketball with my son and not getting tired. That did give me an ounce of satisfaction.

Everyone invited me over for dinner. I didn't want to go anywhere, and I didn't want their dinners. However, I didn't want to be alone either. I hated being alone. I wanted people to come over and do stuff for me. I was basically helpless. I had to have my wife's friend come over to tell me how to wash my clothes. I didn't realize all the things my wife had done. Once it was too late, I realized, in spite of her being tired lately, that she'd done a lot of stuff around the house. In addition, she took such good care of our son, and she worked part time. Every day, I realized more and more how much of a fool I was. I used to think I was a wise and knowledgeable fellow, but now realized I had been a fool.[3]

# How Things Change

*Today, as I sit at my laptop typing, the late afternoon sun shines brightly, but it is cold outside. In Ohio, it doesn't get warm till June. But it is still April. I planted grass a few days ago, so I need to water it often. Although it's only 48°F, the sun dries it out rather quickly. I had to water it twice today.*

*The sun was shining through the den blinds, so I partially closed them. The warmth through the window was nice, but it was too hard to see the computer screen. Isn't it funny? We want the sun to shine but then complain because it is too bright. We want the rain to come but complain it is too dark. We want summer to come, but I guarantee that I will complain when it gets too hot!*

*My son is in his second year of college. My wife is sleeping, I think—I mean, my second wife. She'd had a hard day and had gone to bed early. She'd put in her two-week notice today. She is looking for a new job, as her present one is too hard. Speaking of change, when she started her job less than a year ago, she said it was one of the best jobs at one of the best places she had ever worked. Apparently, things change.*

*In fact, I am working at a different job myself.* I had to move to another state to get it. About eight years after my first wife died, they closed my plant. I had been the IT guy there. The market crashed, which, in turn, forced my plant to close. Actually, we had just built a similar plant in China, expecting the safety-glass film market to expand. However, when the market crashed, the CEO and his team decided to close the more expensive American plant and keep the Chinese people working. How things change. Who would have guessed such a thing would happen back in the seventies when I was going to college. China, the Communist and backward economic giant, is taking our jobs. The real gotcha, however, is that we Americans are the ones causing it. American CEOs of American companies close American plants and lay off American workers and then build them in China so the Chinese can make the products we buy in the United States. If that isn't a paradox, then I don't know what is.

My point is that things change. A boy meets a girl, and they fall in love. He does all kinds of things to please her, and she is always giggly. He says he loves her and asks her to marry him. She says yes, and the wedding day approaches. She goes on a diet. He saves his money for the ring and honeymoon, and they have a wonderful time. Little junior and sweetie come along, and life continues. However, hard times approach, whether financial or emotional. One way or another, the hard times come. Eventually, however, over one-half of these happily married couples fall out of love and divorce. Wow! Did things change! Little junior and sweetie wonder what they did wrong to cause Mommy and Daddy to hate each other. Junior gets mad and begins to get into trouble. Sweetie becomes pregnant. Things change.[4]

I think the majority of these children turn out all right, but not without bruises and hurt.[5] Too often, Mom and Dad just stop trying. Each says the other one changed. I think they both did. One of them should have been preparing for this change and moved to do something about it, but most of the time we expect the other one to do that. We say or believe something like, "After all, I'm a person too! I have feelings! Why don't you do something once in a while?"

Yes, things change. In my previous life, prior to my first wife's death, I had been one of those guys who touched things and they turned to gold. My family was terrific. I was born in southeastern Michigan to a factory worker and a housewife. My siblings were split evenly between boys and girls. I'm the oldest.

I think being the oldest taught me some things. It also made me believe I was better than everyone else. I was the strongest and the smartest of all my siblings. Not that I got great grades or was better than average in athletics, but as a kid, I was stronger and smarter than all of my brothers and sisters. Forget that I was older than them. I was still better. I was the one who took care of the rest of the kids when Mom and Dad had to leave for a minute. I was the one who knew what was best for them. In addition, I was the one who got the new clothes and then handed them down to my brothers. My sister was just fortunate that she got new clothes. However, come to think of it, I didn't get new clothes. I got the new used clothes from my older cousins and so on. Then I passed on those new hand-me-downs to my brothers.

I was fortunate in that my dad wanted me to play the guitar and gave me two years' worth of lessons. He couldn't really afford $2.50 per week, but we kids always got the money before Mom and Dad did. I never remember them buying anything for themselves.

My first real job was at a Roman Catholic Motherhouse. It was the home of the Sisters of the Immaculate Heart of Mary (IHM). My cousin got me the job. We did the dishes, stocked shelves, and mopped floors. We also had many a discussion concerning morals with the older nuns. This job gave me spending money throughout high school.

Once I graduated, I worked at my dad's factory for the summer. I went to college in the fall but dropped out second semester. After quitting college, I went back to my dad's factory. It was a low-paying job and very hard, so I decided to look for another. It didn't take long before a chemical factory picked me up. Again, I was fortunate, because this new job paid twice as much as my dad's factory. It was there that I decided to finish college. I was fortunate, because the company paid for it.

After graduating, I moved into the IT department at the same chemical factory. It was a very good job and paid well. Because of the chemical plant, I was able to afford the house I mentioned earlier. My dad told me I was lucky to have gotten a job at that chemical plant. I arrogantly told him I was not lucky but rather had worked hard to get where I was. I had a good career, because I worked hard and was financially savvy. I was a jerk. My dad was right. I *was* very fortunate.

*While I continue to type, I again look out my den window. The sun is setting. Houses line the street as it winds up the hill dotted with old-fashioned street lights—it's a pretty sight. I am still fortunate. God has given me a beautiful home in a beautiful neighborhood in a beautiful town. Things have changed drastically over the years, but I still am fortunate. And I'm not as arrogant as I used to be.*

# The Dash Counts

*(Flashback -- 13 years ago)*

They wheeled her by with a white sheet from her feet to the top of her head as I sat on the living room couch. At this point in time, I can't really remember what my feelings were. I do know that for the following year, time dragged in slow motion. A day felt like a week, a week a month, and a month was as if it were a year. By the time ten months had gone by, it felt like ten years had passed. My nights were long. They were the worse. I couldn't sleep. Many a night I walked the rooms of my house. I'd wake up thinking I was dreaming when she wasn't lying next to me. I'd smack my face and exclaim, "Wake up!" But nothing happened. I'd then get up, tears streaming down my face, and walk down the hall, through the family room, around through the foyer, and into the living room. I'd make a U-turn and walk through the kitchen and then continue the same process for many laps till I collapsed on the couch and cried myself to sleep. I'd often look into my son's room and thank God he was okay. I promised God that I'd take good care of him and then ask why He decided to take my little son's mom to heaven already. She was only forty-seven. Our son was seven.

We had adopted him seven years earlier in what was one of the most wonderful weekends of our lives. My wife and I couldn't have children. After fourteen years of marriage, we'd finally realized that if we didn't adopt, we'd never have children. So, we went to the Catholic Social Services, which was the adoption agency in our county, and applied for adoption. In the late 1980s, it was very hard to adopt a white baby. I understand it may not be that way today. We could have adopted an older child or a black baby, but we, being white and wanting a child as normally as possible, wanted the same as if we ourselves could have had one naturally. We were therefore put on the waiting list. It was five years long.

It was a rude awakening when we discovered the reality that single women, instead of marrying the man or putting the child up for adoption, were either keeping the child or aborting them. It is a shame that our society is so selfish and does not care what is right for the child. We ought to fall on our knees and ask God to forgive us for seeking what is convenient and easiest at the expense of our children. I would never tell a girl to give up her child if she is not married and the man wants nothing to do with it. I would never tell her to give it up for adoption if she really wants to keep it and can properly care for it. (It is unfortunate that much of the time, however, this minimal proper care is government supported in welfare checks.) However, any woman who aborts her child when there is a five-year waiting list of couples who cannot have their own child and who would adopt a second or third if the state would allow them is an abomination to humanity.

It was a Friday morning when my wife called me at work. She said, "Catholic Services just called, and they have an eight-week-old baby boy! But, the mother was on drugs and drank alcohol, and it's not known yet if the baby has brain damage due to the mother's abuse during pregnancy. And although he was six weeks premature, he has gained some weight back after losing weight at first. What should we do?"

Well, in those days, I was exceptionally wise in my own eyes, although arrogant in others; yet, I was very stable and grounded in what was right and what was wrong. I told her my heart, and to this day, I am proud of my stand. I said, "If God would have allowed us to have our own child, naturally, and when he was born the doctor said, 'He is premature, and we are not sure if he has brain damage,' what would our response be?'"

We both agreed it would be, "Lord, please make our son healthy." And then we'd take him home. So, she called the agency and asked when we could pick him up and bring him home.

I remember that weekend as if it were yesterday. The evening before had been my birthday. What a birthday present! We had gone to see *Jurassic Park*. The following morning, my son was born (to us). God had given us a precious soul to raise. The mother said she wanted her birth child to be raised in a Christian home. She had gone to Pentecostal churches before, so when she found out we did, she selected us. We were next on the list, but apparently, when there are a few people close in time on the list, the agency lets the mother select within certain guidelines. Hence, we were selected. However, she did not know us, and we didn't know her. No names or any information were given out. To this day, I have no clue who she is, and she doesn't know who we are. My son, they said, would be able to find this information when he turned eighteen if he so desired. So far (at age 20), he has not requested it as far as I am aware.

It was Friday and too late to pick him up, said Catholic Services. We'd have to wait till Monday. This was good timing, because we had many preparations to make. I could not think about the adoption during the five-year waiting period for fear that I'd go crazy. Therefore, I pushed it out of my mind the best I could, similar to what I had done during the previous fourteen years we couldn't have children before applying for this adoption. So, when I got home and my wife's smile and mine met, we both said, "Let's get going!"

We hopped in the car and went nursery shopping. We bought a cradle, a baby bed, diapers, formula, wallpaper, paint, and I don't remember what else. What I do remember is working my tail off in the nursery all day Saturday and Sunday. By Sunday afternoon, we had a beautiful nursery and a cradle in our bedroom. The nursery had a baby Disney theme with bright paint on the walls. The crib had Disney characters above it. The room was decked out.

Monday morning, we got up, took a video of our son's new bedroom, and drove to the foster parents' home of six weeks. (Our son had been in the hospital for the first two weeks of his life and then at the foster parents' home the following six.) I remember the foster parents. They appeared to be very nice people with a mixture of many children of various nationalities. An Asian girl was holding our son. She gave him to me. I held him. He was the most beautiful baby boy I had ever seen. I gave him to my wife. She smiled large and long, looking at him, then at me, and then back at him.

We smelled something, so we took him into the bathroom and changed his diaper. I don't think he was more than five minutes old with his new parents before he tested us out. The diaper change was a success, and we took him home. God had given us a son, and during the next seven years, he became more of a blessing as each day passed. In many ways, as you read through these pages, you will see how my first wife's dash was heavy with good.[6]

# But Flowers Still Fade

*It is early on a Saturday morning. The sun is shining. The birds are singing. Because it is also early May, the trees are blooming with blossoms. Color is bursting all over the place. I look into my front yard and see wonderful peach blossoms, crab apple blossoms, and bushes of yellow, ruby, and violet. I walk through my living room and while looking out the side yard window, I see a different variety of crab apple blossoms, pear blossoms, and a tree filled with orchids. The grass is green, the trees are filling out, and spring beauty is everywhere. I continue my morning tour through the kitchen and into the laundry room. Atop of the dryer are eight pots of flowers. Last weekend they were beautiful pink and light violet. Today, I notice, before glancing out the window into my other side yard to admire the blossoming yellow apple tree, that I am stopped by a faded violet and brown set of potted flowers. Just a few days ago they were beautiful. Today, they look like something thrown into the woods out back and left to die.*

Life is full of surprises. Some of these surprises are new and exciting, like the blossoms on my tour above. Some surprises are of lesser value. However, most of life is filled with mediocre. Today, so far, is filled with all three. I've gotten up as normal, made my coffee, and toured my home. I do this most mornings. Of course, most mornings don't have the beauty I saw today. I also saw the faded flowers, which remind me of days gone by. Then, there is the beauty I saw in my yard. I wish I could only experience the beauty, but that is only a sometimes thing. If my yard kept the blossoms on the trees and every day I saw the same things, they would grow old and somewhat mediocre. I don't know if they would meet absolute mediocrity or not, probably not, but they would fade in color and beauty somewhat in my mind. In reality, they would stay the same, but to me, they would not be so pretty and wonderful as they are today. Life is that way. As we grow used to things, they aren't as beautiful as they once were. Surely, they really are, but not to us.

I recall how my first mother-in-law used to look out the window on a snowy winter's day and remark how wonderfully beautiful the trees and the grounds looked. She marveled at how God had made such a beautiful creation. She would elaborate how the snowflakes bounced on the branches of the trees and made such beautiful structures. Sometimes she'd paint these into snow-covered magnificence on the canvas in her living room. However, not long after her elaboration on God's wonderful splendor, the door would swing open and a grumbling old man would enter, slamming the door behind him. He'd look at her and exclaim, "I hate this stuff!" He'd then go on how he had to shovel the walk and driveway and that he'll probably have to dig his car out of the drifts on the way to work. He'd then go on how miserable the snow made his life.

What a contrast. To one person, the snow was a wonderful, uplifting sight of spectacular beauty, but to the other, it was a miserable mess that caused more pain than any goodness it may allow. We all see the same thing but experience things much differently within the midst of it.

Part of the reason for so many differences is due to our own doings. Some are luck and/or good fortune. That in itself is a philosophical paradox. How often could we make our and others' lives more enjoyable by thinking before we act and decide on the best course of action? Concerning the flowers above, had my present wife not gotten upset about an insignificant issue that caused her to go into a temporary state of depression (I will not elaborate as to what caused this, but suffice it to say, she often makes mountains out of molehills), she would have remembered to water the flowers on the dryer and saved them from their dried-up misery. Or, better yet, she could have transplanted them into the pots outside, which was her plan a few days earlier, before creating the mountain mentioned above and going to bed after work and wasting the beautiful days we had. Or, I could have spent two minutes of my time and watered them myself, as I knew she was in no condition to worry about flowers on the dryer. She had bigger fish to fry, or should I say moles to grow into grizzly bears, so to speak. And regarding my in-laws: she could have been more considerate of her husband's burden of snow, and he could have been less cantankerous about having to drive in it. We could all use a bit of beauty training, I suppose.

*I should water these flowers before complaining to my wife about drying them up. I don't think I'll mention the fact that every spring the same thing happens. She buys flowers for the deck and then neglects to water them, and hence, they die off before their time. A good thing to do today would be to water them. I will and shut up about it!*

# Divorce not an option

To my first wife and me, divorce was not an option. We never mentioned it, and we never desired it. Marriage to us was somewhat like siblinghood. When brothers and sisters grow up, they never think of divorcing (or whatever synonym I could use here) each other. They are brothers or sisters for life. That's just the way it is. The same goes with parents and children. Parents may not like what their children are doing. Their child may be a drunkard or a murderer, but they still love that child. They may be disappointed or ashamed, but they still love that child. They are still their children. To us, marriage was that way. Her brothers were my brothers, her parents my parents, and so forth with my parents and siblings. When we said I do, it meant till death.

I once heard Rev. John Hagee on TV talking about his marriage. He said, "Divorce is not in our vocabulary; murder maybe, but not divorce."[7] He was exclaiming the fact that when a man and woman sign a marriage contract, promising to love and cherish each other through riches or poverty, through good times and bad times, until death, that is what they meant. And that meant the contract was binding.

Today's laws concerning no-fault divorce nullify the very contract that couples sign today. It can be broken through such an easy method. Of course, many contracts today can be broken. If you don't pay for your house, you won't go to jail. Rather, the bank takes it away, one way or another. If you stop payment on your car, it can be repossessed (I learned this from the "real TV" programs). Concerning the marriage contract, you just tell the judge you don't love each other anymore, or at least one party tells that to the judge, and he splits the property and children appropriately and life goes on. The marriage contract doesn't really mean until death do us part, but we'll split our possessions if we part.

It is not my purpose to give the philosophical, theological, or psychological reasons for this, as I am not qualified to discuss any of these big three, but I will reminisce as an old fool. After all, this is my book.

My grandfather and grandmother on my dad's side lived together for sixty years. I saw their wedding picture a number of years ago and would swear my grandfather is the mirror image of Leonardo DiCaprio. Of course, when I show my wife and others the picture, they look at it for a moment and say, "Yeah, maybe." But I see DiCaprio when I see my grandfather. Not that he reminds me of him in any other way; I just think he looked like him. My grandfather was born in 1888. Mind you, that was only twenty-three years after the Civil War ended. His dad could have been a child when it ended. Life protrudes into eras, and we don't even realize it. I already told you how he and Grandma greeted us when we "went out home." I have many a fond memory of going to Grandpa and Grandma's farm, way out home. But it wasn't Leonardo DiCaprio and Kate Winslet who greeted us. It was a very old man and old woman who thought the world of us, and we knew it.

My mom's mom and dad experienced quite a different life than my dad's parents. My grandmother's wedding picture shows a flapper wedding gown and cap. I vividly recall the first time I saw it. It was the funniest thing I had ever seen. Well, it was funny because I could never have pictured my grandmother in her early twenties, which would have put her into the late 1920s to early 1930s. My grandfather passed away when my grandmother was only forty years old. They had nine children with the oldest a teenager and the youngest a baby. He was a truck mechanic and was on the road a lot. My mom told me that when he died, it felt to her (fourteen years old at the time) that he had gone on another road trip to fix a truck but never returned.

He had been working on a truck when the jack failed. It fell on his leg. He came home to recover, and the leg looked good and seemed as though he would be fine. Sunday morning, the family went to church and left him home. When they returned, he was dead. The doctor told my grandmother a blood clot from his leg loosened up and went to his heart or lungs, which caused a heart attack. He died immediately.

My grandmother raised their nine children by herself. She cleaned houses and sewed to support them. They continued to attend Catholic grade and high schools and graduated from them. I don't know how she could have afforded the high tuition except she probably got a break. My guess is they let her send them for free, as she was a widow. The Catholic school system was good in that respect. I know my siblings and I went to a Catholic grade school and paid very little tuition because there were so many of us. I know the Catholic parish gave my parents a break, but the break stopped with grade school so we went to public high schools.

I never thought much about it as a child, except that it was much different going to my grandma on my mom's side than it was my dad's parents. It was quieter and cleaner. She lived in the city; my dad's parents on a farm. She didn't have big dinners like my dad's parents, but that may be due to the fact we went to my dad's parents for dinner and my mom's mom had already eaten dinner. It may also have been due to the fact we lived far from my dad's parents but only a few minutes from my mom's mom.

There were millions of grandchildren on both sides of the family. We had fewer things to play with there than we did on the farm. As a rule, though, she seemed less happy. She smiled and was very nice and would do anything for her grandchildren, just like my farmer grandparents, but something was different. My dad always said the French were lovers, and the Germans were bullheaded. I will leave it to you to guess which nationalities he and my mom were. Nonetheless, both sides of the family were happy, and it was always a blast to go to either side for a gathering. But I didn't have a grandpa on my mom's side, so it was quite different.

My plan in this part of the book was to search out a firm position concerning divorce, but I don't know if I can do that. I do know, however, that I didn't have to split holidays with exes. In other words, my parents gave us just one set of grandparents each. There were no hard feelings on either side, and Grandpa and Grandma were either my mom's or my dad's. There was no fussing, just regular normality like our nuclear family.

I guess I could speak on divorce after all. If my parents had been divorced, we would have had to split the deal. We'd go to my dad's side with my dad and to my mom's side with my mom. Then, if they had remarried, we would have more complications with half-grandparents and so on. This would occur every holiday, and there are a lot of holidays. In addition, vacations and other occasions would have become complicated. Add to the fact that we wouldn't see our dad but every couple of weeks and our mom without some weekends. That would have been a major disruption in my childhood.

When my mom's dad died, her mother never remarried. She continued a widow for sixty-two years, dying at age 103. She once told me, while I was looking at those flapper wedding pictures, there was no woman who could ever take her husband from her because she would have fought her off (or something like that, as I can't remember the exact words she used). She was devoted to him even many decades after his death. This dedication appears normal to me, even if she had gotten remarried. The fact she never remarried meant (to me) that she didn't believe in remarriage, which I believe to be the case, or she just never found anyone. If the latter is true, maybe it was due to the fact she had nine kids or because she was always extremely busy with work and the kids. I really think she and those surrounding her didn't believe she should remarry. Her church took care of her. Her siblings brought over food, etc. Their needs were met. Had she married, I know it would have been different, but would it have been as good? Would things have been better? No one will ever know.

# Stepchildren

Children know. They know the difference between a real parent and a stepparent. Now, there are instances where that may not be true, such as when a widower with very young children marries a woman with no children. The woman immediately takes the young children as her own, and then the man and woman have their own children. If the woman is careful, she can treat them all the same. I know of an instance like this, and from conversations from one of the children of the widower, the family melded fine. This child told me he missed his mother dearly; she died giving birth to twins when he was only seven years old. Yet, his love for his stepmom was great, and because he and his siblings were very young when she came along, the family became a normal family. The "real" children were treated by the parents equal to the stepchildren. He told me once that the words *step* and *real* were not allowed in their vocabulary.

I see the opposite in my situation. After my wife died, my son didn't really grieve after his twenty-minute I-want-my-mommy episode when I told him his mom was in heaven. Oh, I haven't gotten to that part yet? I will.

The day after my wife died, our son had a soccer game. This seven-year-old boy had a soccer game, and he was not going to miss it. So, my pastor, his family, and I went to his game. He did well. At the funeral home, he ran around and cut up with the other kids. At first, I told him to settle down, but I soon figured it was good for him to be a kid, even at his mom's wake. The funeral was different, but the wake was somewhat of a good time for him.

After the funeral, I decided to buy a double tombstone with my name beside hers and our son's name on the back, stating that he was our son. The days dragged on like weeks, the weeks like months, and the months felt like years. Ten months after my wife's death, I met this beautiful girl at church. She came into the library looking for a specific book. As I was the church librarian, I helped her look for one. In the course of conversation, before I realized it, we had talked all through the first service. We heard the singing when the lobby doors opened and were amazed we'd missed the church service. Then I blurted out, "Want to go to dinner this afternoon?" Her face brightened like an angel, and while nodding her head, she agreed through her big smile.

My son was always in the habit of either going to a friend's house after church or having a friend come over to our house. Even after his mom died, we continued the tradition. This time, however, there was no discussion; he went home with a friend. I took the pretty blonde out that afternoon. Three months later, I put a wedding band on her finger. I know this all seems quick, but to me it felt like it had been ten years since my wife had passed away and three years while dating my wife.

I told my new wife she was Help from the book *Pilgrim's Progress* by John Bunyan.[8] She had pulled me out of the quicksand when I was up to my ears in mire yelling, "Help! Help! Help!" She pulled me out, cleaned me off, and made me into a new man. God had smiled upon me and given me a new start. For ten years (actually, ten months) I was as Job in the Old Testament of the Bible who had lost everything. Now I was a renewed Job. Life was good again.

This was the woman God had given me for taking my first one to heaven. My first wife was in heaven. She had received her reward for making her "dash count." She was a good Christian, a wonderful wife, and the best mother to our son. I had missed her dearly, dreadfully dearly. Words cannot describe the horrendous misery I had been in for ten months. Now, all of that was past. God had looked down upon me and said, "Now, you shall enjoy life and be miserable no more." But that's not how my son saw things.

# I Want My Mommy!

After meeting my present wife on that Sunday morning and taking her to dinner, I asked her to come to the house the following Tuesday evening. I had two motives. I already knew she was the one—actually, the second one, but that is a difficult thing to explain to someone who has never been a remarried widower.

I loved my wife who had passed on to heaven. But she was dead. For ten months/years (I sometimes use the months/years term to explain real time/perceived time), I had tried to talk to her. I tried to touch her. I tried to love her and have her love me back. But there was no response. When I said, "Honey, what do you think about this?" there was no answer. When I said, "Our son is adorable, isn't he?" I didn't hear her voice. When I reached over to touch her, I only felt air. I couldn't love her except to feel my heart ripping out of my chest. It wasn't ripped out, because that could heal. It was ripping out. The pain was excruciating and unexplainable. My agony was beyond explanation.

C.S. Lewis, in his book *A Grief Observed*, which he wrote after the death of his wife, said grief felt like fear. He wasn't actually afraid after the death of his wife, but he had the sensation of being afraid. He also said that through his grieving period he had excessive laziness. The slightest effort was exhausting, or rather, he just didn't have the ambition to initiate anything. And not only was he grieving terribly, but he spent all of his time thinking about grieving terribly.

He was correct. I don't believe anyone who has never lost a loving spouse can understand what he said, but I know it is true. It was a feeling I had never experienced before. I couldn't eat. I couldn't think. I couldn't work. I was fortunate I had an employer who saw beyond my work ethic at that time and into my misery. Otherwise, I would have been fired. I couldn't concentrate. When I did try, I would spin into a dizzy spell. I ended up in the hospital the first two times and in an ambulance the third. I soon learned to stop thinking before this happened, because throwing up while spinning in circles is not very fun. My job consisted of concentrating on various aspects of technology. Because I could not do that very deeply, my production faltered. Then, to add to that problem, I had no ambition or energy. I wonder to this day how I kept my job. The grace of God is my only explanation.

At any rate, my second motive for inviting her to the house was that I needed to know how she and my son would get along. He was now eight years old. For the past ten months, he had been just fine. I couldn't figure it out. I dragged myself to bed, out of bed, to work, to church, to family functions, and on vacation (for my son). He, however, seemed happy as a jaybird.

Anyway, she came over, as sparkling and as beautiful as she had been two days earlier. I cooked boneless, skinless chicken breasts with mushrooms and mozzarella cheese on the grill with baked potatoes on the side. It was a hit.

Afterward, since it was winter in Michigan, we decided to play basement baseball.

There are two things to consider concerning baseball in the basement. Not long before my son was born, I fixed up the basement with paneling, a drop ceiling, and carpet. It was thirty-one feet by sixty feet, so it made a fairly good baseball stadium for an eight-year-old boy. Second, my son's passion, if you didn't figure it out already, was sports. It didn't matter which one; as long as there was a ball involved, he was in. On his second birthday (Or was it his first?) I got him a mini basketball net and a basketball. My wife in heaven (I call her "mom in heaven" for my son) took videos of him shaking the ball and walking toward the net saying, "dribble, dribble." He then dunked the ball. As the ball swished inside the net, he shouted, "Shoot!" Ever since he was four years old, he'd ask me to go to the mailbox and get the newspaper so he could find out "who won all the games" the night before. He'd reach for the sports section, glance at the pictures, try to make out the headlines, and ask if he was interpreting the scores properly with the proper team. His exclamation, "Daddy, who won all the games?" rings in my head to this day.

He had the rubber bases in place in the basement, and with plastic bat in hand, he asked me to pitch him the Nerf ball. My new girl was the outfielder. We all had an absolute blast playing basement baseball. Hitting the lights was an out. If you hit the ball over the Ping-Pong table, it was a home run.

After exhausting my girl and I, we all went upstairs to the living room and sat down to watch TV. My girl and I sat on the couch together, but my son wanted to sit across the room on the love seat. Things seemed to be going so well. I thought, *Wow! God has given me a girl to take me out of my misery, and my son loves her!*

It was around ten o'clock that night, and it looked like my son was sleeping. I reached over and gave her a quick kiss on the cheek. Suddenly, without notice, he started to cry. My son was not sleeping! Hysterically, he began to exclaim, "I want my mommy. I want my mommy. I want my mommy." He had now begun the grieving process for the death of his mother.

# Is Life Just a Crapshoot?

After my wife died, I would tell people that God throws everyone into a bucket. When it's time for a trial or hard times, he stirs us up and, while closing His eyes, reaches into the bucket and pulls someone out. He looks at that person and says, "Okay, it's your turn!" But that was not my philosophy before her death.

For decades, I believed that everything was under God's control, that He determined what would happen to everyone. Life or death was not determined by a crapshoot or luck but divine providence! He sees deep into our future and foreordains what happens in our lives with the utmost skill and precision. Every hair that drops from our heads is predetermined and ordained by God. I didn't know why some people's lives were rough and others not. I knew, even then, that some very good people were going through very hard times and some very bad people were experiencing exuberance in life. I didn't understand that, but God was in control! He knew what He was doing and did what was best in our lives. I didn't try to make sense of it. My life was, on a scale of one to ten, probably nine and a half. Why God was so good to me, I didn't know. He just was. Why wasn't God so good to the hungry in Ethiopia? I didn't know the answer to that question either. God had everything under control. Then, my wife died.

# No, No, No!

I was at work on Thursday afternoon when I received a call. It was my wife. I thought it was strange, because she never called me at work. She said she was very sick and wanted me to come home. I knew the flu was going around. After all, it was winter in Michigan. She said she wanted me to stop at the pharmacy on the way home and pick up this new drink they had that shortened the span of the flu. I didn't have anything unusually important going on at work that required me to stay, so I told her I'd be home in a little while. I mentioned to my coworker I was going home because my wife had the flu and she wanted me to come home early. He said he and his wife had the bug just weeks earlier, and it was the most horrific flu they had ever had in their lives. He said it was terrible, and they'd felt pressure on their chests. His wife said she thought she was going to die. We both chuckled.

I headed to the pharmacy and picked up the medicine. I told the pharmacist my wife felt pressure on her chest and was very sick. He said, "Yes, that's the type going around this winter."

When I got home, I gave her the medicine. She said she felt like she was going to die and had pressure on her chest.

I didn't chuckle this time, as I could tell she was very sick. I told her that was the type of flu going around according to the pharmacist and my coworker. I then went into my den and began studying for the New Testament class I was teaching that evening.

My pastor and I had just started classes and hoped to turn them into a Bible College one day. Certainly, for the time being, we just enjoyed teaching those who wanted to learn. That evening, in addition to lecturing, I was giving my students an exam. My wife begged me not to go to class but to instead stay home with her. Since she was vomiting, we had to watch that she didn't go too long without her hormones. As mentioned earlier, because none of her glands were functioning, she had to take all hormones orally. If she continued to throw up, I would have to give her a shot. I had never done that before and was not looking forward to it. Her doctor told us she could go three days without her pills but no more. It was always our plan that if she got sick and could not keep them down for more than a day, I would call her doctor. It looked like that day may have come.

I told her I needed to give my students an exam and would come home afterward and bypass my lecture. She begged me again not to go, so I told her I'd run the exam to my pastor, who would proxy the exam, and I would come right back home. She agreed. When I got to the church (our classes were held in the Sunday school rooms), I handed the exams to Pastor and told him the story of my wife's sickness. I kiddingly held my hands up as if they were a balance and told him I was weighing the importance of my wife compared with the school but couldn't come to a decision. I said I'd still better give him the exams to proxy and head back home. He laughed and said he'd take care of the exam and I'd better get back home. I did.

The following morning, my wife was still feeling terrible, but she'd stopped vomiting her hormone pills. She asked me to get some mandarin oranges on my way back home after dropping our son off to school. I said to her, "Good. The medicine must be working, and I won't need to give you that shot."

Our son began walking toward her to give her a kiss and hug, but she said, "Don't come any closer, Son; I don't want you to get this flu."

I thought it a bit strange but only figured the flu was as terrible as she had been letting on. I dropped our son off at school and went into the store to purchase the can of fruit. While there, I saw a minister's wife I knew. I told her my wife had the flu and felt terrible but it appeared she was getting better since she was no longer vomiting. We talked for a bit, and I then proceeded home.

I gave my wife the oranges, but she didn't want them. I told her she needed to eat, so I spoon fed her. It reminded me a bit of when she couldn't move the first time she got sick and ended up in ICU. I now became concerned, thinking that although she was not vomiting her hormones, she was still not getting better. Nonetheless, I figured it was because she hadn't kept her medication down for almost a day now and that was why she is so weak; plus, she had the flu. To be safe, I told her I would call her doctor. When I contacted his office, the nurse said he was busy but would call me right back.

The night before, my pastor told me he was asked to speak at the local high school concerning teens and suicide.

One of the school's students had committed suicide not too long before that. Because I was the church librarian, he asked me if I could do some research on the topic for him. So, I began studying the topic and wrote down some points for his speech. I noticed about forty-five minutes had passed, and my wife's doctor still hadn't called back. When I talked to the nurse again, she said she'd make sure he called me back.

I went into the bedroom to tell my wife. As I spoke, she looked still as death. Feeling a little concerned but not fearing anything terrible, I went around to the other side of the bed. Her face looked very white and still. I began to shake her as I whispered, "Honey." As I moved my hand toward her arm, I noticed it was somewhat bluish. And when I touched it, it was ice cold. I shook her and exclaimed, "Honey!" She didn't make a move.

My heart now began to beat fast, but I still was sure she was just cold and sleeping and very sick. When she still didn't respond, I yelled louder, "Honey!" I shook her hard. When there was still no response, I began doing CPR, not believing she was dead. She must have just stopped breathing, which caused her heart to stop, but I was sure I'd get it started again. I had just talked to her forty-five minutes earlier! She just had the flu, for crying out loud! She was no longer vomiting her pills, and the pharmacist and my coworker and his wife said pressure on the chest during this flu season was not abnormal.

My mind began racing. *I just talked to her a little while ago! I need to get her breathing again! I need to get her heart pumping!*

I had taken first aid and CPR classes because I was on the emergency response team at the chemical plant. I was confident she would be up and talking soon. I did three heart compressions … three deep breaths … three heart compressions … three deep breaths … three heart compressions … three deep breaths. Pause. There was still no breathing. There was still no heartbeat.

I opened her mouth wide and noted some food in her airway (I didn't think of this till later, but apparently it was the orange I had fed her), so I cleared it out and began breathing into her mouth again and saw that her chest was rising. After a few more breaths, I gave her heart compressions again. I rotated these back and forth a few times and then called 911 while continuing the CPR routine. The person at the other end of the line told me to move her off the water bed and onto the floor. He said I could do a better job there. Still not thinking she was really dead but had only temporarily stopped breathing, I continued CPR while awaiting the ambulance.

At one point, I heard a crack while doing chest compressions and told the paramedic on the phone, "I think I broke her rib!"

He just said, "That's okay. Keep giving CPR. The ambulance is on its way."

Now I was beginning to lose hope, but not entirely, so I kept performing CPR while praying to God to give her breath. Suddenly, I heard someone at the door. "Praise God! The medics are here!" I ran to the door. It was my dad.

I looked out to the driveway and said, "Where's the ambulance?!"

He told me he didn't know but explained that my sister-in-law had heard the call on her emergency radio and called him, so he came over as fast as he could. I asked him to watch for the ambulance and ran back to the bedroom and resumed CPR while praying my guts out. Finally, I looked up, and the paramedics were standing behind me.

"Well, get down there and start working on her," I said as I stood to my feet.

They looked at each other for a moment and then began CPR with their equipment. Behind the paramedics stood two sheriff's deputies. I left the bedroom and began walking up and down the hall. Each time I came to the end of the hall where the bedroom was, I walked in and asked if she was breathing yet. I'd proceed from the bedroom, down the hall, to the family room, and into the kitchen. I'd then go back into the family room, down the hall, and into the bedroom again. I was crying, praying, and chanting that God would bring her back. I must have looked, acted, and sounded like a medicine man praying for the sick while the white doctor worked on his loved one on one of those old Western TV shows.

I was finally beginning to think she was really dead at this point, but I still knew God could bring her back. I don't really remember if I thought He'd actually bring her back to life, but I kept saying God must heal her and bring her back to me. This time, when I walked down the hall and into the bedroom, the door was closed. I opened it and then saw the two paramedics and the sheriff's deputies standing around my wife. They were talking, and she was still dead.

I yelled in a loud and hysterical voice, "What are you doing? Get working on her!"

The deputy looked at me sternly and while closing the door said, "You need to stay out of here, sir; we are treating this as a homicide."

For a brief second, I had three thoughts run through my brain. One: *She isn't dead!* Two: *Get working on her!* And three: *Homicide?!* If I hadn't been in so much torment, I would have laid that deputy down flat so he *could* accuse me of homicide.

I continued to rant and holler and pray till I finally realized the inevitable. "My wife is dead. My wife is dead. My wife is dead. I can't believe it. My wife is dead." I stood in the living room with my dad. Soon after my mad medicine man dance, I called my pastor.

I said, "My wife is dead."

He replied, "What?"

I said, "My wife is dead."

He was at the house within a short time.

I either stood or sat in the living room; I don't recall which. They rolled her body down the hall and through the living room. A white sheet was covering her, head and all. They rolled her out the front door, down the sidewalk, and into the driveway. They pushed her into the ambulance. I stood at the front door and then on the porch. They drove out of the driveway and then down the road. My wife was gone. My wife was dead. Now, I had to tell my son and also her parents.

# The Stone

My dad, mom, and pastor were in the living room when the ambulance drove away. I don't remember anything between that time and when the pastor and I drove to my wife's parents. I think not much time had lapsed. It must have been around noon or so, on a cold winter's Friday. I don't remember my specific feelings at that time very well anymore. I do know, however, that from that day forward, till I met my present wife, I was very numb. My feelings were very inward. I had to force myself to do anything that would be of benefit to anyone else. I do know I couldn't do much for myself. A few days afterward, I remember my sister-in-law showing me how to load, put in soap, and turn on the clothes' washer. I had never washed clothes before. (I had to be shown again later, by my wife's friend, as I had forgotten some things—I was a mess.) I couldn't even concentrate hard enough to figure out that simple task.

I know this numbness and unconcern for others did continue for many months. Seven months later, the September 11 terrorist attack took place. I recall everyone in my office scurrying about while listening to the radio. They also had newscasts playing on the TV in the conference room. Women were crying, and everyone was at high alert.

I remember very well wondering what all the fuss was about. As I watched the tower burning on TV, another plane ran into the second tower. I went back to my desk and marveled that everyone was so concerned. It was just a couple of burning buildings that some lunatics ran airplanes into. *So what?!* I thought. *Events like that happen all the time! Why is everyone so hysterical?*

I look back now and think, *Wow, I was an idiot! I couldn't see the atrocity of such an event?* I was stone-cold numb and unconcerned for anyone else. I was too numb to be concerned for other people.

I now wonder if that is how thieves and murderers feel. I wonder if various events in their lives have caused them to become stone-cold numb and excessively unconcerned for others. How else could a man kill another for one hundred dollars cash in a register? Why would anyone steal money from someone who is barely surviving on social security? What else can cause a man to swing a bat and beat another man to death for no good reason? People like that have no concern for others.

Did the murdering thief's dad leave him when he was a child? Was his mother on drugs and showed no concern for him as he grew up? Did he have to fend for himself all of his life? To survive, did he have to beat out everyone else for his daily food? Was he around hate and torment every day of his life? Did he only see selfishness and poverty around him and throughout his neighborhood? This, I think, could cause a man to become numb to others' feelings.

After many years of abuse, from a small child then on into his teen years, this hate would increase. As he hates more and more, it becomes easier to hate. Was it the numbness of life that caused him to hate? I don't know. I'm just thinking on paper.

During my period of numbness, I didn't harm anyone; I didn't want to. I didn't lash out at others, and I didn't wish anyone any harm. Maybe it was because I was brought up in a good household, and that tradition continued after I was married. However, I was certainly mad. I was mad at God. I was mad at my wife for dying and leaving me with our seven-year-old boy to raise alone. It wasn't that I did not want to raise him. It was that he was now without a mother.

As a child in the 1960s, I recall a TV program called *Divorce Court*. For some reason, my dad watched it. I think it may have been about the time his nephew, who was his age, divorced and remarried. Either way, in that era, divorce was uncommon. I wasn't aware of anyone who was divorced. (As a child, I didn't know my cousin had divorced.) I do remember the program scaring the heebie-jeebies out of me, though.

I remember wondering, *Why do couple's divorce? What if Mom and Dad divorced? What would I do?* I don't think I thought it out any further than, *What would I do?* But I did extend it into other options. Options like, *What if Mom died?* I recall thinking of my mom or dad dying, but I think I hated the idea of Mom dying more. I love my dad just as much as my mom. I would have been torn to shreds if either parent were to die. However, I guess because Dad was at work a lot but Mom was "always" at home, if she died, it may have been harder for me. I'm not sure.

Now I still wonder about kids whose parents split up. What do they do? How do they handle it? How much more work is it for the parents to make sure the kids know they love them and that the divorce is not the children's fault?

When my wife died, I thought I had killed her. It seemed the autopsy took forever. But that cannot be so, as the funeral was only a few days after she had died. Nonetheless, I considered myself a murderer for not taking her to the emergency room the very first day she was sick. I kept saying to myself, *What an idiot! Why didn't I take her to the emergency room Thursday evening instead of going to that stupid New Testament class?! She may only have had the flu, but she also had that hormone disorder. Sure, the doctor told me she had three days before having to take the needle, but the flu, causing more stress, may have accelerated her need for it. She did stop vomiting the following morning, so why did she die? The doctors had told us she would live a normal life since she was taking the hormones orally. It doesn't make sense! I killed her!*

When the autopsy finally came back (I believe the actual report came out a few days after her funeral), the pastor told me he'd take me to the autopsy office. The doctor told us my wife had contracted a bacterium that is virtually always eliminated by the immune system. However, because my wife had a weak immune system, she was not able to fight it off. In addition, she may have actually contacted the flu, which would have weakened her body even more. He said the pressure on her chest was due to the bacteria she'd contracted. This bacteria caused a peanut buttery-type substance (for lack of a better layman's term) to surround her heart. This constricted the heart's functionality. Hence, the pressure in the chest and excessive weakness, as her blood was not flowing properly. If she had not contracted the flu, the reason for her vomiting was due to the fact that when women, unlike men, have heart problems, the nerves affect the stomach and can cause vomiting-type symptoms. Therefore, the next morning when she stopped vomiting, it was not due to her getting better as I thought was happening, but rather to the fact that her stomach was empty from vomiting and her not eating. Finally, the heart continued to constrict more and more until it quit beating.

When we left the office, my pastor said something to the effect that it was not my fault and her death was due to the description just received from the autopsy doctor. I felt a bit better but then soon realized, although I did not kill her, I was negligent for not taking her to the hospital. If I had, they probably could have saved her. My Internet research, which consumed me for the next few days, made me realize this bacterium could have been conquered with antibiotics.

In this case, the physicians would have poked a hole in her chest cavity and inserted a small tube through it. Through the tube would drip antibiotics directly onto the heart. This would have killed the bacteria fairly quickly. I should have taken her to the hospital, and they would have saved her. She would not have died if I had cared more for her than I did that stupid class and the antisuicide paper I was researching for my pastor. Because of me, she is lying under a stone. For the longest time I felt that way. To this day, many years later, I don't entirely disagree.

# Twenty Minutes of Grieving

After the paramedics wheeled my wife's body out of the house, my pastor and I went to her parents to give them the news. They both just sat there. This was one of the hardest things I have ever done. I had to force myself to do my duty.

During the next ten months, my whole life was a regiment where I forced myself to do my duty. I didn't want to live. One day, while on my way to work, my eyes were filled with tears, as they always were when I was alone. As I neared the railroad tracks, I didn't notice the guardrails coming down even though lights were flashing and bells were ringing. Just before I got to the tracks, I slammed on my breaks, finally realizing the commotion just ahead was a train traveling around thirty miles per hour. When I finally stopped, the rail was at my bumper. I thought to myself, *It doesn't matter that I stopped or if I hadn't stopped.* I really didn't care to live anymore. I didn't want to kill myself. I just didn't like living. The only thing that kept me going was my son. I promised God and myself that I would take good care of him, whatever it took.

Speaking of which, because we always had a vacation every summer, I promised my son that would continue. To partially get out of it, however, I told him our vacation this year would be a three-day trip to the Cedar Point Amusement Park and we would stay at Hotel Breakers on the grounds. Under normal circumstances, it would have been a magnificent short trip. In fact, it was to my son and his buddy. But to me, it was drudgery. Coming out of the hotel, we were greeted by cascades and waterslides. In the hotel was a huge pool. Just across the way were roller coasters and other amusements. But to me, it was no fun. Nonetheless, I had to give my son a vacation, and as far as he was concerned, the fake smile I kept on my face, although actually an upside down frown, was good enough. I forced myself to smile. I forced myself to give my son a good time.

How often in life must we force ourselves to do the right thing? In family situations, friendships, and work relationships, we must sometimes force ourselves to do what must be done. We must do it for the benefit of others, certainly not for ourselves. The cherished teaching of Jesus Christ, "Do unto others what you would want others to do unto you," should be fulfilled often in this life.

I sometimes wonder how often my dad and mom did the same for me. Parents do that for their children, partly from instinct but mostly because we actually love them. It is a state of being that is hard to explain. That child who is part of us from birth is an extension of our own lives. Although having a separate body and mind and often a different way of thinking, we cannot let loose of the fact that he is our child. "That is my son" is a phrase with horrendous meaning. What he does is of utmost importance to me. His sustenance is my responsibility, and I am happy about that.

One of my students stopped me in the hallway the other day and exclaimed, "My little boy is crawling now!" She was smiling from ear to ear as she showed me videos on her smartphone of him crawling. She and her husband made a little boy. They are a part of him. We wouldn't take a million dollars for our children. Of course, some children may take a million dollars for their parents, but that's a different story.

I don't know why exactly, but at least during certain periods of a child's life, parents aren't as cherished as are children. Even as children mature and become adults, the parents still worry about them and continuously think about them. I don't think children do that with their parents. My dad is always telling me to come over once in a while. I am always telling my son to come home from college and visit once in a while. I don't visit my parents as often as I should, and my son doesn't visit me as often as he should.

As my pastor and I sat on the chairs in my in-laws' living room, they sat on the couch across the room. They had sensed something terrible had happened. Forcing the words the best I could, I told them their daughter had passed away. "She had already stopped breathing when I went into the bedroom to talk to her. I gave her CPR and tried to revive her. The ambulance came and tried also. We thought she just had the flu. I don't know why this happened."

We all continued to sit there silently. Then her dad said, "I knew she was really sick. I saw the ambulance traveling toward your house while on my way to the post office to mail her Valentine's Day card this morning."

My heart stopped again. I don't recall what else transpired, except that the pastor spoke to them for a bit. I think I just sat there in dreadful pain. I can't remember if her mom cried or not. Then, the pastor and I left for home to prepare to tell my son the news.

I never thought of it till now, but I wonder what her parents did after the pastor and I left that chilling afternoon. My guess is they probably held each other and wept till they ran out of tears. Then what did they do? Did they go to bed? Did they get on the phone and call their relatives? Did they talk? Probably, they just sat there staring at the wall or out the window, silently, wondering how this could have happened and what they were going to do now that their precious, youngest child, and only daughter was gone.

That day wasn't the first time parents were devastated by the sudden death of their child. It wasn't the first day a young wife was suddenly taken from the arms of her loving husband. That dreadful, winter's day was not the first time a mother was taken from a small child. But it was the first time my wife had ever been taken from me. It was the first time my in-laws had lost a child. It was the first time my son had lost his mommy. And this was the first time we had been devastated by an event that shook and ended our world.

"I drive his truck,"[9] is a phrase from a country song that was popular not long ago. It tells the story of a father who drives his son's truck (or a brother who drives his sibling's truck). He drives it to get as close to his son as he possibly can. His son was killed while serving his country in the military. The song basically describes how a father is devastated by his son's death and begs for his son's presence again. But he is not there, only his truck.

For months after my wife's death, I would visit her grave. I'd sit on the ground and stare at the stone. Tears would pour from my eyes. My brain would hurt from the strain. It was a strange feeling. If you have ever laughed so hard you couldn't breathe, you may be able to understand the sensation. However, think of an opposite feeling, one where you can't breathe, as in deep laughing, but with a frown, a crunched nose, and tears streaming from your eyes. It is as if you are forcing everything out of your head but nothing is there to force out. You just feel like your head is going to burst out of your forehead. You can breathe, but it is difficult.

I could have brought dinner to the grave and enjoyed eating it there. It wasn't morbid, spooky, or haunting. It was a natural feeling to be there. I wanted to be there. I was more comfortable at the graveyard than at home or at a friend's or at church. I was only six feet from her when I was standing upon her grave. However, I did sometimes wonder if she had started to decay. But again, I was not fearful of such thoughts. She was not really there anyway. She was in heaven. In fact, I often thought about how she got the best end of the deal. She was in heaven with her beloved grandmother, Jesus, the angels, and I was stuck here under the burden of my lost wife and my son who will now have to live without his mommy. My arms had been taken off; I had no brain. I was a miserable mess.

# You're My Mommy Now!

Around three thirty in the afternoon on the day my wife went to heaven, my mom picked my son up from school. I saw them walk into the living room. My son could sense something was wrong. The pastor was there; my dad and some of my brothers and sisters were sitting with me in the family room. My son gave me a kiss and hug. I stopped him as he began to walk toward the bedroom to greet his mommy.

Putting him on my lap, I said, "Buddy, Mommy is in heaven now. She is very happy. We will see her again in heaven, but it will be a long time before that happens."

He looked at me and began to cry. At first it was a light cry, and then it became louder. Finally, at the top of his lungs, he cried, "I want my mommy," over and over and over again for what I believe was about twenty minutes. As I rocked him on my lap, he continued to bellow out, "I want my mommy!"

My friends and family sat in grief, watching the episode. After a few minutes, I took him into the bathroom. We sat on the bathtub step while he screamed, "I want my mommy!" Finally, he stopped, and just as suddenly, while looking up at me he said in a calm voice, "That's all right, Daddy. Now you are my mommy and my daddy."

I still heave with pain from my chest and on into my throat when I think of this. I picked him up and walked into the living room. He never cried another tear over his mommy *until* that day I kissed his "new mom."

# I'll Fix You Dinner

For a few months after her death, I didn't have to do much cooking. It was a good thing. Sure, I could cook steaks, burgers, and chicken on the grill. For breakfast, bacon and eggs were my staple. To fix anything else, I'd have Bob Evans or Applebee's do it. Not to worry, I had offers coming from the woodwork. Female cousins I hadn't seen in years brought dinner to me. The neighbor ladies made me casseroles and dishes I had never had before. People from my church invited my son and me over for dinner. My mom and mother-in-law fixed meals whenever these other friends and family did not. I was eating high on the hog, literally.

However, I didn't want the fancy dinners and the company that went along with them. I had to force myself to get ready and go to these gourmet feasts. I'd rather have ordered pizza and watch TV with my son. My son and I would go to the video store and rent a movie and eat fast food on the few days I wasn't given a dinner offer. My best movie to watch, when my son didn't talk me into another one of his sports movies, was *Shadowlands*[10] starring Anthony Hopkins as C.S. Lewis. It's the story of a portion of C.S. Lewis's life when he met a spirited young lady from the United States. He married her and then experienced her death. I saw this movie for the first time when my wife was still alive. I told her, and others, that it was the best movie I had ever seen. It was a real tearjerker.

Lewis was the chair of Medieval and Renaissance literature at Cambridge University and a popular author when he met this woman with Communist tendencies. He didn't much care for that part of her but did admire the spirited and academic conversations he had with her. Eventually, they were married. While together, Lewis's wife contracted bone cancer. Then it looked as though she may have been healed by God (she was in remission), and life was good. She had two sons before she met Lewis, but the movie only recognized one. It looked like he was around nine years old. After not too much time went by, she had a reoccurrence of the disease and died. C.S. Lewis then raised her boys.

But the part that jerked my tears occurred soon after her death. Lewis became a very bitter man. He could not understand how God could take his new bride away. After all this time, he finally met his wife, then she contracted cancer, and then she went into remission! All appeared to go well, till … wham! She wasn't healed after all but instead died! Sure, he knew she had really been in remission, but the disease resumed and she died! The ending scene showed Lewis and his stepson sitting together, thinking about her, both helpless, hopeless, and crying their eyes out. Little did I know, that would be my son and I only a couple of short years later.

# "She Was ..."

Before my wife died, one of the favorite pastimes my son and I had was to sit on the couch and eat crème sticks while watching TV. We had a ritual that went like this. When we ran out of milk or some other groceries, I'd run to the party store down the road. Quite often, I'd say to my son, "Let's go to the store, bud," and we'd hop in the car and go. While at the party store, we'd pass through the pastry department. Whenever our coveted crème sticks by Nicolas's Bakery were in stock, I'd get a pack. While picking it up, he'd smile and say, "Don't tell Mommy!" and we'd both laugh as I sneakily put them into the basket. Once home, the ritual continued.

I'd wait till my wife was out of the kitchen, and he'd watch me put them into the back of the cupboard, acting as if that was a spot my wife never went into. While doing so, I'd smile and say to my son, "Now don't tell Mommy!" We'd both giggle and then move into our daily duties or hobbies or whatever we may have been doing that day. Usually, if it was warm out, we'd go outside and play ball. If it was cold out, we'd go down into the basement and play ball. If it was late or he had already worn me out playing ball, we'd turn the TV on and watch ball! It was then that we knew it was time to enter the vault that was in the shape of a cupboard, reach in, and pull out our cherished treasure.

In the evening while the TV was playing our (my son's) favorite program and my wife was in one of the other rooms, it was time to move. We'd look at each other and say, "We don't have much time; she'll be back soon. Let's move!" We'd sneak into the forbidden gardens (actually, it was the kitchen). He'd stand guard, while I opened the vault. Delicately, I'd reach in, being careful not to touch any of the insignificant objects that surrounded the treat, like vegetables, grains, and vitamins, and slowly pull out our treasure and close back the hatch.

I'd look at my partner and say, "Is the coast clear?"

He'd respond, "The coast is clear."

We'd proceed, very quietly, from the forbidden gardens, through the dark forest (foyer near the family room), and into our paradise (living room). After sitting down with a glass of milk and plenty of napkins, we'd delicately open our treasure. I'd give one golden nugget to my partner and three to myself. We'd giggle as we bit down into our Nicolas's Bakery crème stick delights. Sometimes, we'd hear rustles in the forest.

"It's Mom! Yikes, hide the evidence!… It's too late! Oh no, we've been found out!"

Our beloved enemy would look at us sternly. Then her face would brighten, and with the biggest smile you've ever seen, she'd say, "What are you two doing?" We'd all laugh and talk about how we'd been caught again.

We had many games we played over and over again. One of our favorite movies was *Home Alone*. We'd put up with the first half of the film and then have our kicks with the slapstick second half. Every time Kevin slapped the aftershave on, we'd slap our cheeks and exclaim, "Ahhhhhhhh!" When the robbers slipped, fell, and got "scammed by the kindergartener," we'd laugh as if it was the first time we had seen it.

But after my wife's death, *Home Alone*, Nicolas's Bakery crème sticks, and baseball weren't the same. Sure, I'd force myself to get the crème sticks, but "she" was no longer around to catch us and keep us in suspense. *Home Alone*, wasn't funny anymore, and basketball and baseball? They turned into a real chore for me.

I used to coach my son's Little League baseball team. After my wife's passing, I wanted to give it up, but the head coach said he was short on coaches. If I quit, they would probably have to cancel the league that summer. So, I coached my son's team again. Because I couldn't concentrate, my eight-year-old took on the unofficial responsibilities of assistant coach. He was a born leader anyway, and this was his opportunity to "lord it over" his fellow teammates. I look back now and have to imagine the parents wondering what was going on. But that wasn't the worse of it. I often found myself, trying to "snap out of it" and remember which team was at bat and which team was on base! I recall one time seeing the runner make it safe to first base, I yelled, "Good job!" while clapping my hands. Then I heard my players' parents in the background exclaiming, "What? He cheers on the other team's players?" I realized what had happened and felt like a fool. I tried to save face, but that was impossible. It was a miserable time, but I had to do it for my son.

My wife was a gift from God, but God took her away. She had left me my son but took my heart when she left. I often told my boy that if it weren't for him, I didn't know what I'd do. I told my pastor and friends that if it weren't for my son, I'd be spending my evenings in the bars. He is all that kept me sane. However, I was barely sane.

# God Gives. God Takes Away.

When I came into work today *(while still in the midst of writing this book)*, I had an email from a guy I used to work with. Attached to it was an essay my son wrote when he was in junior high school. The essay read as follows:

> <u>Death</u>
>
> It was just a regular day at school, until my Grandpa and Grandma picked me up after school instead of my dad. When I got home, I saw my Pastor's truck in our driveway. At first, I thought he was just over to visit my mom. So I ran as fast as I could to see him but when I got inside my dad said we had to talk. He said, "My mom had passed away."
>
> At first, I just stared at him for a couple of seconds, and then started crying my eyes out for twenty straight minutes. Then, I took him in the bath and told him I would be all right.
>
> Many people came over to spend time with me and my dad. That was probably my favorite part of this tragedy. In addition, Pastor and his family spent the night with us a lot. That was fun because I had people to play outside with and play Playstation with. Then we got

> all kinds of food and dishes but we ended up throwing most of the stuff away.
>
> My mom passed away on February 9, 2001 because there was fluid trapped around her heart. I still miss her to this day but now I have a new mom [*my present wife.*] and two brothers [*my present wife's sons*]. I still have my dad who helped me through that tough year.
>
> My mom and dad are the two best parents a kid could ever ask for.

My old work acquaintance travels to the manufacturing facility I had been laid off from (during the market crash, spoken of earlier—a very small facility is still kept there) periodically to work on the network there. He resides at the Massachusetts facility but comes to Michigan quarterly. I had apparently left this essay on my desk when I left, and he had just gotten around to scanning and sending it to me.

The plant closing was a hard time for me. I thought God would give me an easy life after my wife died. After all, wasn't that enough? Wasn't it enough that I had to deal with all that pain and suffering? Apparently, it was not.

Because the economy was so bad, especially in southeastern Michigan, I couldn't find work. For almost two years, I sat around smoking cigars. Sure, it was a nice break, but I didn't know how I was going to make my house payments and maintain everything else. Then my present (second) wife, being very stressed out, decided to leave me [*this is the first time my present wife left me, approximately 4 years ago*]. She left for one and a half years. However, after I finally landed a job in Ohio, she came back. I sold the house in Michigan and bought one in Ohio. We made a new start. The money wasn't as good as it used to be, but it still wasn't bad for a technical teacher. Teachers don't make as much money as businessmen, but I loved my job. My wife worked also. Things were good but different than they used to be.

In the end, I realized that I am no better than Job, who lived a few thousand years ago, when he said, "Naked I came out of my mother's womb, and naked shall I return thither: the LORD gave, and the LORD hath taken away; blessed be the name of the LORD" (Job 1:21; KJV). If someone whom God said was a good and just man can lose everything, I am no better. I just needed to realize that this side of heaven, anything can happen, at any time. We just need to try and be ready the best we can.

*While sitting at my desk, continuing to write this book, I ponder, my son.* He is my pride and joy. He's a junior in college with a baseball and academic scholarship. Don't worry; it is only a partial one. Believe you me, I still have a hefty sum to pay. This is a sore spot with my present (second) wife. She could give her sons nothing while they were growing up. When I first met her, her sons were grown. One was twenty-four and working for a lawn service, the other was twenty-one and a waiter at a local restaurant. Her younger son still lived at home. The oldest, although single, had a house trailer.

My son was only eight when she and I met. I had always promised him I'd send him to college. This hurts her, as she could not do the same for her boys. But I can't send them to college too. After all, they were adults when I first met them! I don't blame her for not liking the idea that I am paying for my son's college education, but what can I do?

# PART II

# She Left Me Again

I have just decided to divide this book into two parts. My initial intent was to reminisce about my life with my first wife and complain about how I should have treated people differently. One of the reasons was because I could look back at my past fifty-nine years and reflect on how I could have done some things better. However, toward the end of part one, you may have noticed a slight turn in my style. It was written just days before my present wife left me again.

I had promised myself that I would not make the same mistakes with my second wife that I made with my first. However, my second wife has serious psychological issues that I have had to deal with since we married almost twelve years ago. I had treated her very well and loved her dearly. However, she has made it very difficult. Right after I had written the end of part one, the day after Mother's Day, she left. Over the course of our last few weeks together, I had a feeling she may be getting ready to leave again, but I had no idea it would be so quick and abrupt. Since I've not been able to concentrate since Mother's Day and could not see as I was crying my eyeballs out every day, I have not touched this book in approximately nine months. I still can't believe it. I will now shift gears and talk of my second wife.

# It Was the Happiest Day of Her Life

She (my 2nd wife) was fourteen years old. Her dad called her into his hospital room. He said, “I am sorry.” She didn’t believe him. The next day, he died. That day was the happiest day of her life.

From the time my wife can remember, she had a terrible childhood. Her dad was a Pentecostal preacher and ruled the family with an iron hand. (Now, what I am about to tell you can happen in any religious group, nationality, or ethnic group. I will not put down Pentecostal preachers. The most Christlike men I have ever known were Pentecostal pastors. I am only condemning what should be condemned.)

Her family went to church every Sunday, both morning and evening. They also attended the midweek youth service. In addition, because her dad was a preacher (but not a pastor), they went to many revivals. Needless to say, church was a major staple in their household.

Her parents had eleven children all together. My wife was in the middle. The family had no television, because entertainment was a tool of the devil. They did not believe in drinking, smoking, playing cards, being involved in sports, or watching theater. But there was a deep, dark secret that the preacher man kept concealed.

He didn't like my wife. He called her big nose (which, after she struck out on her own, she had fixed. She now has the looks of a super model). He beat her. Sometimes he stripped her nude and made her run around the load-bearing pole in the basement. As she passed by, he'd whip her with his belt. Sometimes he'd force her into the closet with no water after making her drink hot sauce. Other times, he'd make her scratch his fat, stinky feet as he rested on the couch. It wasn't unusual for her to be sent to bed without supper. She hated her dad.

She told me how every evening her dad would sit her blonde sister (who was one year her elder) on his lap and stroke her hair and talk sweetly to her. But to my wife, he'd talk rough. When she sought his attention, he'd tell her to get away. Her childhood was hell. My wife often commented how she couldn't understand why her mom didn't stop him, but she loved her mom anyway. In fact, she misses her mom terribly. Her mother's passing a few years ago is one of the reasons she had a hard time, again, this past Mother's Day. It's complicated.

After her dad died, she was in bliss. However, another dreadful interlude in hell was just around the corner. I did not know this till just a few years ago, but she had an extreme trauma not long after her dad died. Her oldest brother forced her to have sex with him. He raped her over and over again. If she didn't give in, he'd beat her. Her mom was often away at work, so he held the family reins. This trauma, along with her father's abuse, gave her issues, to say the least.

I think if such things had happened to me, I'd have turned into a drug addict or an alcoholic bum. But not her;

she prayed and fasted and went to church. She still does. However, the satanic abuse she received has taken its toll. She is now extremely paranoid and worries excessively about what others think of her. She is especially concerned what I think of her. If I glance at a girl, she thinks I want that girl and that she is not good enough for me. She continuously told me I don't think she is pretty and that I do not love her. Without perpetual adoration and attention, she'd think she was not loved. Her father and oldest brother took care of that. Those bastards!

Twelve years ago, when she first met me, she said she was in heavenly bliss. I would often tell her how beautiful she was and how much I loved her. I didn't know she needed constant attention; I just enjoyed telling her. Before we married, I had no clue she would be jealous of anything. But after we were married, if she saw a pretty girl within eyeshot, she immediately lost hope and thought I didn't love her. After so many years of this I became very weary and stopped telling her I was sorry for looking at these girls. During our early marriage, I did say I was sorry. I didn't understand what was going on and didn't know what else to do. I began to tell her she was hallucinating. She didn't like that at all. Because I didn't praise her beauty as much as I used to, in her eyes, my armor began to fade. In fact, I gradually became a scheming villain who sent the dragons to her instead of defending her from them. She lived in black and white. To my wife, there were no grey areas.

One Sunday (approximately two months before she left me this time) I decided to go to a different church than her, mainly because she was having another one of her "episodes" and partly because I always wanted to see what a Mennonite church service was like. There are lots of Mennonites and Amish in the Akron area and figured I'd visit their Sunday morning worship service. When she asked me why, I told her I wanted nothing to do with her type of Christianity (meaning, of course, the way she was acting—but, as is usually the case, she misunderstood an otherwise obvious comment and thought I didn't like her church). She began to weep bitterly. When I melted in her presence again (as my heart always tears out when she has one of these weeping episodes), I told her I'd go to church with her after all. So, she was in very good spirits again. We went to a nice dinner afterward. It was a very good day. But the previous week had been dark and devious.

She had accused me of looking up the neighbor's skirt as I was cutting the grass. It was just another in a long line of stories she told me. If she would have gotten mad and forgot about it, it wouldn't have been so bad (I did not look at the neighbor lady; my wife only thought I did), but she persistently shunned me and slept in the spare bedroom for a few days. Hence, my comment to her about not wanting anything to do with her type of Christianity.

# The Episodes become More Frequent

The morning following the Sunday incident, my wife went to work. I had an evening class, so I didn't get home till late that night. I came into the dark bedroom thinking she was asleep. Before I reached the bed, with anger in her voice, she said, "Why were you rummaging through my desk drawers?!" I told her I hadn't. She continued to call me a liar and accused me of looking at her things. I was the villain again who was now trying to mess with her head.

Our short but heavenly ride was over, again. I was put back into hell. I again said she was mistaken and told her to go to sleep. She became even angrier and moved to the spare bedroom. I just laid there wondering what in the world was going on. I knew, however, she was losing it again and that it would be a matter of time before she snapped. But, I figured I had some time to figure out what to do. In the meantime, I would try to walk gently.

A few days later, she was fine again. It was the Saturday before Mother's Day. My stepson texted me saying flowers were being sent. If we were not home when they were delivered, the florist would call my wife. I was so excited, as my wife always loved it when her sons sent her flowers. It was a much needed gesture at the present time, because she was having so many episodes so close together. At eight thirty that evening, I thought it strange the flowers had not yet arrived, so I checked the front porch. Sure enough, they were sitting by the door in a box. I called for my wife to come to the door, but she was in the bedroom and asked me to bring them up. After opening them, she asked if I would cut the stems. I said, "Honey, your son sent these to you. Enjoy them for a bit before going to bed. She got mad as a hornet, marched down to the kitchen, and cut the stems. She then slept in the spare bedroom again.

The next day she told me her hands were hurting, and that's why she had wanted me to cut the stems. Had I known, I wouldn't have told her to do it herself. This was a classic example of her turning a mole hill into a mountain. I could never learn when the hill would start growing till after it turned into Mount Everest. Therefore, this small mishap turned into a major issue, which, by the way, had been the story of my life for the past twelve years.

It was Mother's Day. She left early in the morning for her last day at her job. I drove three hours to my parents' home for their sixtieth wedding anniversary and then three hours back home. When I arrived home around five o'clock that evening, I told my wife to get ready for our dinner date as we had planned. Looking very disgruntled, she said, "I already ate!"

Because I had cut my visit short with my family, whom I don't see much of any more, to take my wife to dinner for Mother's Day, I quickly asked why she was so mad. Suddenly, she threw her laptop at me and said, "You are always wrecking my Mother's Day!" She ran into the bathroom, locked the door, and began to sob horrifically. I tried to talk her into opening the door, but she would not. She slept in the spare bedroom again that night.

The following evening she was not there when I came home from work. She wouldn't reply to my calls or texts all day until I texted her after getting home that night. She replied, saying she went to her son's place three hours away, in Michigan. I haven't seen her since. It has been nine months. To this day, she will not answer any of my calls or texts. In fact, a couple of months ago, I received a letter from her attorney stating I was not to contact her. She had moved to Florida.

# Those Bastards!

I recall watching a *General Hospital* episode many years ago. During that particular season, the show dwelt on the fact that one of the stars had been raped. Because of this trauma, she wouldn't sustain a close relationship with her husband. She continuously pushed him away. I recall very vividly wondering why she would do such a thing. At least, best I can remember, her husband was a kind and loving man, who was doing everything he could to try and help her. He loved her dearly. But instead of accepting that help, she did not want him near her. It appeared as if she blamed him for something someone else had done. I was dumbfounded and just wrote it off as a dumb soap opera that had nothing to do with real life. Today, however, I see the reality of it. Because I had never experienced anything like that, I thought her behavior was impossible. However, the past twelve years have proven *General Hospital* to be prophetic in my life.

My wife's father and oldest brother, of whom I fondly refer to as, bastard and bastard junior, destroyed my wife's life and, by proxy, have nearly destroyed mine. I have had bad times due to varying circumstances, but my wife had been destroyed by people who were supposed to be her loving support. During her youngest years, as she was experiencing what life was about, she only encountered torment and horror. She didn't laugh or smile. She only saw her older and pretty sister (more on that later) loved by the very man who made her life a ride across the River Styx to the land of Hades. Then, when Cerberus (the three-headed dog guarding Hades—bastard) finally died, she had to fight Medusa (the snake-haired demigoddess from Hades—bastard junior) and her ferocious monsters. To be honest, in spite of her problems and constant distress, I don't know how she grew up to be such a pretty and sweet woman. Her dark side shows, that it true, but when she is not troubled by her *General Hospital* rape-victim mentality, she is a goddess.

# If I Only Had a Brain

We could learn something from the scarecrow in *The Wizard of Oz*. He said he didn't have a brain, but he was the wisest and most knowledgeable of the three strange characters. He and Dorothy figured things out. The Tin Man and the Lion followed along. Sometimes we overthink things. The scarecrow, in his simplicity, was a wise ole crow. He had common sense.

One of the things that moved our nation forward and into the Revolutionary War was common sense. Thomas Paine asked why a people should pay excessive taxes to a king on the other side of the ocean when he wouldn't let them represent themselves. The king of England made the rules, which were detrimental to the colonists, and then they paid him large portions of their income. In his pamphlet *Common Sense*, he challenged, in plain and simple English, the authority of Britain.[11] People understood him. He made common sense. He didn't overthink things, at least not in his writings to the common people.

Often, we overthink and get ourselves into trouble. Let me use your job as an example. Let's say your boss always wears a frown. It's easy to draw the conclusion that he is an old grump and hates everyone's guts. In reality, however, maybe his child is sick or his wife died. In my early career, I had a boss who never smiled. I also noticed he'd go into his boss's office and call his wife every lunch break (this was before cell phones). I thought he was a grouchy mush. Then one day I saw him lowering his wife from their specially designed van. She was in a wheelchair. He was smiling. He had many worries concerning her health and his ability to pay for the additional equipment. He called her every lunch hour to ensure she was okay.

Certainly, in this instance with my boss, I thought too deep. I jumped to a conclusion. Too often, we jump to conclusions or overthink situations. Sometimes we try to figure out what is going on without any facts. As youngsters, our teachers taught us that first impressions are usually wrong. But, although we know we shouldn't, we continue to rely on first impressions.

As husbands and wives, we have empirical evidence that first impressions are entirely incorrect. Once we get used to each other, we begin to take our guards down and reveal who we really are. This "real" person is sometimes nothing like the person we first met.

My wife is much different than I thought she was before I married her. (However, I do recall some things that should have tipped me off.) In like manner, I am different than I was when I first met my wife. The problem is, I don't really know much about that. And she doesn't know how she has changed. She thinks she's the same. I think I'm the same. This is where our brains and common sense come into play.

Common sense tells us that we see the change in the other but not in ourselves. Therefore, if we use our brains, we should try to find out what has changed within ourselves.

After all, we do know we are no better than our spouses. Once we figure out some of these changes, we should try to make the appropriate modifications to improve ourselves. But instead of doing this, we always try to change the other person. We then get mad because they are different, when, in fact, our own changes may have caused the other person to change and vice versa.

I know it sounds like I am trying to make you think too much in this chapter when I said, "Don't overthink." My point is, let's use common sense to determine what the real problem is (that would be ourselves) and then use our brains to work it out. Use common sense. "Do to others what you would have them do to you" (Matt. 7:12 ESV) Or, if you prefer the negative version, "Don't do to others what you don't want others to do to you."[12]

Very often in a marriage, and I know from two of them now, when your partner begins to let his or her guard down, you begin to do so also. Add to this the fact that, usually, although you are not aware of it, you have already begun to let your guard down. So, when you continue to do so, you have now let more guard down than you intended. Basically, after we are married awhile, we get sloppy. This takes me to my next point.

Our expectations sometimes increase as our mates begin to let down more and more of their guard. In simple terms, we expect much from our partners, while we are doing less for our partners. When we date or are married for only a short time, we let the idiosyncrasies of our partners pass by, either without notice, or at least without saying anything. We continue to put more and more of our partner's idiosyncrasies into our pockets until, one day, we pull them out and—poof—they explode. The guy who was so gentle and said nothing of his wife's idiosyncrasies in the past is now suddenly ranting and raging about them. Yes, it is true; he just couldn't take it anymore, but she doesn't see it that way. She, who may not even know she has these idiosyncrasies, only sees a soft-spoken gentleman turned into a raging monster. Hence, as he is yelling at her, she sees a monster. He may be trying to reason with her, but with his high volume, she only hears hateful noise. He comes out of the argument hoping he knocked some sense into her skull, while she comes out thinking she married a Dr. Jekyll and Mr. Hyde. Both husband and wife lose a battle that was fought for naught. Often, the battle leaves scars that may never go away. Of course, with minor differences, the wife may have been the instigator and the husband the receiver. Either way, both now wear scars.

My present experience has left me empty, without brain, without heart, and without hope. But because I also experienced this a couple of years ago (*speaking of the first time she left me*), I am now much better to withstand it. For nine years, I had put up with false accusations until one day I got so mad that I asked her why she stuck around if it was so bad. I had no idea she would actually leave, but she did. I was so dumbfounded I didn't know what to do.

My son, who was then entering into his senior year in high school, had grown to dislike her because of her hallucinations. She blamed him for things he didn't do. He also sensed how she favored her two boys over him. It was obvious to both of us. (In fairness, although her two boys were adults when I met her, I now look back and think I may have done something similar. But my son was only eight years old when we met!) I begged her to come back for a year. Finally, she agreed, but only if we bought a house in Ohio. My son's heart was broken when I sold our house in Michigan. I had built that house with my own hands, but the girl I built it for was lying in a graveyard.

My present wife and I were going to make a new start. My son was now in college, so we moved him into the dorm. Things were going pretty good for about a year or so, till she began to go haywire again. Sure, I didn't do everything perfect, but did I do anything worthy of divorce? Not at all! But she only thinks in black and white. To her, a person is either a saint or a demon. In my wife's mind, there is nothing in between.

# What Do I Do Now?

What is my next step? I can't beg her to come back again. When my first wife died, I was devastated. When my present (second) wife left me the first time, I was devastated but not nearly as much as when my first wife died. This time, I am even less taken aback. It is true that I don't like it, but as an old man can withstand pain better than a child, I am beginning to stand instead of fall when the wind blows.

I recall as a youngster my dad coming into the house rather quickly with his handkerchief on this wrist. Blood was dripping onto the floor. He told my mom to get a towel and some peroxide. In those days, my dad thought peroxide cured everything. He wasn't as bad as Toula's dad in *My Big Fat Greek Wedding* with his Windex,[13] but it was close. I remember it vividly. As he was cleaning his hand off and pouring on peroxide, I asked what he'd done. He said he was drilling in the garage, and it slipped and drilled his hand. I looked at his face; although it was stern, he did not cry. I thought, *Wow! I'd be crying my eyeballs out!*

We get used to pain as we grow older, and our tolerance level toward others also becomes shorter. Again, using my dad as an example: I recall as a kid being able to make a pretty good mess in the house before my mom would "yell" at us. My dad thought nothing of it. Today, however, if the great-grandkids look as though they may begin to make a mess, he'll tell them to "Take it outside." His tolerance for others is much lower than when he was younger. This is normal. A psychologist once told me[14] that there is something in the brain that, as people mature, changes and causes them to not care as much about what others think of them; therefore, they don't hesitate to give their opinions.

I suppose this is true of mental anguish and heartache also. I don't know if it is due to a chemical mental state of the mind, but it's certainly true in my case. "Time heals," is a popular expression. I would add to that, "Repetition strengthens the heart's immune system."

# Another Turn

A couple of weeks after my wife left me, I noticed a bit more space in the entrance way from the back door when I came home from work. I looked up and realized the hanging plant was missing. I thought, *She's come back home and is watering her plant!* I was so excited.

Then, through the half wall, I saw an empty living room. The couch, love seat, La-Z-Boy chair, end tables, and trees were gone. My guts sank. My heart and my whole insides felt like they were falling out. I thought, *She is gone for good.* It wasn't the worse feeling I'd ever felt, but it was gut-wrenching, nonetheless.

When my wife died thirteen years earlier, I felt like I went to the grave with her. Four years ago, when my present wife left me the first time, I felt a terrible pain, much worse than I feel today, but not as bad as when my first wife died. As mentioned earlier, my intent in writing this book was to speak of my pain and misery after my first wife's death, not my trials and tribulations due to my present wife's actions. However, the pages have taken a different turn. My present situation is a surprise to me. In the midst of writing my book, my wife had gotten back to her old ways, of which I was hoping against hope were a thing of the past. But, my misery persists. I sometimes wonder if purgatory is real, and it exists on earth.

My pain today is truncated and numbing. I won't bore you now (see part III) with the details as to how every one of our vacations had been ruined because she said I wanted the girl in the restaurant or desired one she sighted on the beach. I won't mention now her constant surveillance to see who I was looking at when I was outside or watching the TV. I won't yet detail how she hit the recall button on the TV remote to see what I had watched while she was away for the day. I won't elaborate how many times she told me I didn't love her because I didn't get her the proper gift for her birthday or because I didn't fall down at her feet and worship her that day. Or when I stared at her (of which I did often, admiring her beauty) how she thought I was trying to pick out flaws on her face. If I told her she was the most beautiful girl in the world, she would smile and enjoy the comment. But if I forget to say it, she thought she was ugly that day. For those of you who read this and write off my comments as one who just didn't pay attention to his wife, you are wrong. She had a serious case of narcissism to say the least. But, I won't bore you with any more details, at least not for the moment.

# Life's Lessons

Wise people learn from their mistakes and misfortunes. You can judge me from this book. I've had a few lessons, some of which you've read about already. I learned that sometimes God smiles upon us and sends good fortune. Such occurred when I was nineteen years old and He sent me my first wife. She was so kind and gentle. He smiled at me again when He gave me salvation.

My first wife was Pentecostal. If you know anything about Pentecostals, at least the old-style ones, you know they get a bit wild during their worship services. They go to church on Wednesday evenings, sometimes on Saturday evenings, and always twice on Sunday. The minister preaches at high volume as he tells his congregation to live right or they will go to hell. The congregation sometimes becomes so excited they run around the pews and shout the praises of God. Although I've enjoyed and agreed with what the preachers said, I never did like their high volume. Concerning running and shouting, I don't care for that either, but I understand how excited people get when they think about what awaits them in heaven. My first wife and I never ran the aisles or shouted like that, but we were constant church goers and enjoyed its people. God gave me His salvation and my wife too.

He smiled upon us again, after nineteen years, by giving us a son. Before that, God gave me an excellent job at a major chemical factory only a couple of years after I married my first wife. Life was very good. I was then able to finish my degree and land a technical job at the plant. I was also director of information technology at a local hospital. It appeared God was always smiling upon me. Never as much as a frown came down from heaven. Certainly, there were trials and tribulations (one was when my wife was sick but then diagnosed and healed as far as we were concerned). And there was the fact that we had to wait nineteen years for our son, but God came through. We just had to wait.

But waiting is hard.

> … they that wait upon the LORD shall renew *their* strength; they shall mount up with wings as eagles; they shall run, and not be weary; they shall walk, and not faint. (Isa. 40:31; KJV)

I recall this song we used to sing in church. It was taken from the Old Testament book of Isaiah. It's fun singing about waiting, but it's hard to do. It reminds me of working out or dieting. We get together with friends and talk about the foods we ought to eat and the exercise we ought to do. It's such enjoyable conversation. However, when it comes to eating all of our vegetables and lifting weights or running, it's another story. It's difficult to diet and exercise.

I find it very hard to wait. I sit in pain, wondering what my present wife's next move will be. I am confident we are through. Not only is the living room furniture gone but also the furniture from the dining room, her den, and the spare bedroom, as well as all of her clothes and belongings, the curtains, pictures, and plants. She even went through the stuff in the basement and took the Christmas decorations. It is now February. I am confident we will divorce. Our final trial is April 3. Unless she comes to me crying and begging forgiveness, I can't take her back, even though I want to so bad. She will just leave me again.

My son and his girlfriend came over Memorial Day weekend. They were surprised when they saw all the room I had in the house. It was terrible. I'd rather exercise and eat lettuce. In fact, as I continue my nightmare, I am afraid I'll be eating bread and water when it's over.

# Hypocrisies

Before reading the following sentences, I'd like to make it known that I do not claim to be any less hypocritical than anyone else. With that said, I do know of some hypocrisies that many people maintain. Take drinking and smoking for example. Some people believe it is a sin to drink alcohol or smoke cigarettes. I don't entirely disagree with that. It is tough to believe there is anything like smoking in moderation. Any amount of smoking, whether it be cigarettes or cigars, is harmful to you and those who come into contact with the smoke. But to call it a sin I believe is too rigid. In many, if not most cases, the same individual who believes it is a sin to smoke does not consider gluttony a sin. To be honest, the Bible does speak of gluttony as sin[15] but does not say smoking is a sin. Gluttony is also one of the seven deadly sins.[16] Of course, tobacco is a new-world crop and therefore was not known in Bible times or the Middle Ages.[17] But, I think I agree with many in that smoking should be similar to gluttony. Both are harmful to our bodies and also to others around us in varying ways. (A smoker may die before his time and therefore cause pain and suffering to his family, so the glutton may suffer from diabetes and other complications and hence relegates much pain to his family.) Nonetheless, we do need food but do not need cigarettes. So you could easily argue my logic.

I also think it a hypocrisy to say drinking beer and wine is wrong. Some people, including my present wife, believe drinking a beer is worse than getting a divorce. This kind of thinking I attribute to a terrible misunderstanding of moderation. It is important to be moderate in all things.[18] Aristotle discusses this in his *Nicomachean Ethics*.[19] Americans sometimes think of the abuse of alcohol as drinking. Certainly in the old west, it was thoroughly abused. Many a saloon was filled with gambling drunkards who later went upstairs to a Prostitute. In some places, it was common for a husband to come home drunk and beat his wife and children. According to the *Roots of Prohibition* by Detroit Public TV,

> By 1830, the average American over 15 years old consumed nearly seven gallons of pure alcohol a year—three times as much as we drink today—and alcohol abuse (primarily by men) was wreaking havoc on the lives of many, particularly in an age when women had few legal rights and were utterly dependent on their husbands for sustenance and support. [20]

These kinds of circumstances helped feed the temperance movement, which eventually led to prohibition in the early twentieth century.[21] The preaching of moderation evolved into the preaching of abstinence. Abstinence preaching then culminated into abstinence by law. Abstinence did have inroads in the British Isles and other parts of Europe, but Prohibition was mostly, but not entirely, an American phenomenon.[22] The taming of America was the instigator.

Certainly, the cause was noble. In fact, many churches climbed onto the bandwagon, and new denominations emerged in response to this or at least embraced the idea and made it a part of their doctrine. The Pentecostal church we belonged to was one of these churches.

However, doctrinally speaking, the Bible is clear that drinking wine is a normal part of life. Wine was to be drunk in moderation, but it was never denied a good part of mankind's diet. Jesus and the apostles drank wine. Noah drank wine. So did Lot. Certainly, Noah and Lot did not always drink it in moderation, but drink it they did. Jews drank wine. Jesus made wine. So did my dad. Of course, the wine Jesus made was better.[23]

During the time of the New Testament, wine was a staple of the Jewish diet. Children even drank a watered-down version, as did many adults. The point is, alcoholic beverages were common in Bible times, and Jesus and His followers drank it. It is wrong for a church to teach more than what Jesus Himself taught. We can be stricter on ourselves than Jesus told us to be, but we cannot force it on others. His apostles tell us to drink wine in moderation. They do not tell us not to drink wine. Mohammed did that.

Islam is a corrupt form of Christianity, Judaism, and Paganism.[24] Islam considers wine a sin. (Islam also believes eating pork is a sin, which is a reversion to Judaism.[25]) Christianity taught no such thing until the temperance movement of the nineteenth century, and that was predominately in the United States. The fruit of the vine is healthy when taken in moderation. But do we need wine? Of course not. Do we need chocolate cake? No, but let's not forbid it.

The writings of the Church fathers, mediaeval scholastics, Reformation theologians, and the Bible are silent concerning abstinence of alcohol except for special purposes. The claim that drinking beer or wine is a sin is new.[26] It is hypocritical and false.[27] It is certainly commendable for Christians not to drink wine, but it should not be forbidden. Beer as a form of alcoholic beverage falls into the same category as wine (made with grains instead of fruit). Whiskey, however, may be exempt from my logic because of its extreme alcoholic content, but I will not delve into that.

Divorce is another story entirely. Jesus and His apostles were clear on this. The Christian Church from its earliest stages declared divorce to be a sin. Exceptions did persist, but they were minimal. Jesus says that if your spouse dies or commits adultery, you can remarry.[28] That was about it. The apostle Paul appears to state that if your spouse deserts you, you can divorce, but I'm not sure about remarriage in this instance.[29] The Reformers in the sixteenth century did teach that you can remarry if your spouse deserts you.[30] The Roman Catholic Church, however, only allows remarriage after the death of the spouse. The bottom line is that the Christian Church has never allowed remarriage except in cases of the death, adultery, or desertion of the spouse. It is unfortunate, however, that many of today's Protestants allow divorce and remarriage if the spouse looks at someone wrong, or if they don't like beer.

# The Saga Continues

It has been a number of weeks since I've written anything. A lot has happened. My attorney was elected judge. I now have another attorney. I'm not sure how he'll work out. The laws are pretty fixed, I'm finding out. No matter who is at fault, the income is divided with no questions asked. My attorney had to calm me down when I was surprised by a letter I received stating they would be pulling alimony out of my check starting this week. Although my wife stole around $75,000 worth of cash, belongings, and equity, it doesn't matter. That will have to be determined in the final court, which is due in about a month. Hopefully, that will end everything, and I won't get robbed, although I am sure I will.

I finally finished my MBA. Once the divorce proceedings are complete, I'll begin looking for a new job. I don't want to get one that pays better till then, as a percent of my income will be withdrawn. This is very unfair, but the no-fault divorce laws don't care. My wife has left me for no good reason, yet the courts will force me to pay until I'm at the poverty level to keep her financially fit.

Why do so many women leave their husbands today? It's an epidemic. Society preaches that woman can have what they want. Certainly, marriages, when they get old, are not as romantic as many would like. So, some women divorce and try again with someone else. After all, she can extract half his assets and his pay (even if she deserves none of them and deserts him for no cause). By the time the alimony wears out, she'll find someone else. Or maybe she'll try a career. She has many choices. It's too easy. It should not be that easy to destroy someone else's life. Certainly, society did well in liberating woman from rogues of men who despised and depressed them. However, it is now casting men aside.

Society wants to be 100 percent sure women are no longer trampled on. It has some merit, but it tramples the hearts, minds, and souls of innocent victims. I'm not speaking of men and women who truly do the other one wrong. I'm speaking of the court system that embraces such atrocities.[31] My present wife has stolen my son's college education fund, is demanding half my pay, and is causing me excessive misery. Never mind the fact that she had nothing when I married her. That doesn't matter. She claims I abused her the day before she left. She is a liar and a thief.

# Once upon a Time

I spoke earlier in this book about how the Lord took my precious wife from me and a mother from my son, not to mention a daughter from her parents. When she died, my son was okay, temporarily. My parents were devastated. Everyone loved my sweet wife, the perfect wife and mother, the wonderful church secretary. When they wheeled her across the living room in front of me with a white sheet over her head and body, my world all but ended. My son kept me going, but survival was all it could be called. A survival of misery is what it was. I have spoken of my first life that died with my wife. Now I will continue with my second life.

# PART III

## My Second Love

# Once upon a Second Time

She is poison. That's what my attorney told me. I called him this morning asking why I need to start paying alimony before the pretrial date. He only replied, "You need to quit asking her back!"

Just last week I sent him an e-mail telling him to tell her attorney to tell my wife to come back home. Then I got the alimony letter. My attorney said I need to calm down and quit asking her back, because she is poison. She *is* poison, but it sure did taste good going down. It's like drinking too much wine. It tastes so good at first, and then it feels so wonderful. However, in the morning, the hangover makes you realize that along with that nutritious grape comes the alcoholic poison. That is my present (second) wife. Here's my other story.

## Help

> Wherefore Christian was left to tumble in the Slough of Despond alone; but still he endeavored to struggle to that side of the slough that was farthest from his own house, and next to the wicket-gate; the which he did, but could not get out because of the burden that

> was upon his back: but I beheld in my dream, that a man came to him, whose name was Help, and asked him what he did there.
>
> Sir, said Christian, I was bid to go this way by a man called Evangelist, who directed me also to yonder gate, that I might escape the wrath to come. And as I was going thither, I fell in here.
>
> Then Help said, But why did not you look for the steps?
>
> Christian replied, Fear followed me so hard that I fled the next way, and fell in.
>
> Then, said he (Help), Give me thine hand: so he gave him his hand, and he drew him out, Psalm 40:2, and he set him upon sound ground, and bid him go on his way.
>
> *Pilgrim's Progress*, by John Bunyan.[32]

On February 10, 2001, I felt like Christian in the passage above. Burdened down and carrying a heavy load. I felt like I was in quicksand, going deeper and deeper down. Then, on December 10, 2002, only ten months later, Help came. She gave me her hand and pulled me out of the miry clay. Help had long blonde hair and a slender, five feet eight, 125-pound body. Her face was the prettiest I had ever seen. Her smile was prettier than any angel I had ever seen a picture of. Her voice was also angelic. She said yes when I asked her to dinner.

We were in the church library, but I already talked about that earlier—how we hit it off so well, and she came over for dinner the following evening and she, myself, and my son played baseball, and, well, my son started to cry when I kissed her. But now I will talk of us—her and me.

Over the next three months, we talked about our wedding day. We set the date for March 16, 2002. Yes, only three months later. But she was the one. I would kid the younger folks not to do what I was doing, but I had to marry her in such a hurry because we didn't have much time left. After all, I was forty-seven, and she was forty-three.

By this stage in my life, I was pretty well set financially. I had around $200,000 in a 401k and was saving for my eight-year-old son's college education. I had a very good paying job as an IT systems analyst at a major chemical company. My pay scale was in the upper level for IT folks, roughly that of a chemical or electrical engineer. I had a lucrative retirement plan. I also had a lot of gold and silver. My house would be paid off in nine short years (by the time my son went to college), and I had plenty of money to spare. I was proud of this and made sure my new wife was aware of it. As she had been poverty stricken much of her life I, as her new savior, would give her everything she deserved. I had worked very hard all of my life, and since Help had come, it was time I enjoyed life.

In 1986, I have already mentioned I built a house with my own hands. It was a beauty. There was a seven-by-sixteen-foot brick fireplace in the family room with cathedral ceilings. Large beams held up the knotty pine ceiling boards. It proceeded into the foyer and then into a living room with fifteen-foot ceilings. Attached to the foyer was my pride and joy: glass French doors as you entered a den with wall-to-wall, floor-to-ceiling bookshelves, which I made myself. These shelves were filled with books, most of which I had read, barring the encyclopedic sets. Many of them were of church history. These, and others from college libraries, I used to write my first book in 1995. It was a history of the church from the time of the apostles to the ending of the major Church Councils.[33] I was a proud man. Although the book was jointly published (at least that's what the publisher told me, although I think self-published would be closer to the truth), I was proud of it. I must have sold a thousand copies! Some were to bookstores and libraries. It is in the Library of Congress (I am sure stuffed away in its musty basement somewhere). It was not a success, but I was proud of it anyway.

I was now going to give my new wife, who then lived in a house trailer, a beautiful home. She was gaining a husband who was a well-established professional (a published professional!) who would pull her from her miserable past and into a princess drama. Prince Charming had found her slipper and was preparing to put it on her foot. Or, as she and I used to kid around, I was a knight in shining armor who saved the damsel in distress. And she was Help who pulled me from the miry clay.

Along with this dream home (that I had actually built for my deceased wife), I also had a new car and a Harley Davidson motorcycle with a sidecar. She had an older vehicle and owed more than it was worth. She had no savings or assets, only bills. But, I was happy to fix all of that. God had finally blessed me beyond my wildest dreams, and I was good for it.

After we had dated for a couple of weeks, and my son continued to either play on his PlayStation in the other room or go into his bedroom since he did not like her, I realized I needed to make an honest woman out of her. She went to prayer meetings every week in addition to revivals and many of the other services at our church. As holiness Pentecostals, we both believed in living holy, but she was much more Pentecostal than I was. I believed the apostle Paul made it clear to the Corinthians[34] that if the members spoke in tongues and shouted about every Sunday that visitors would not come back, for they would think they were crazy. So, I thought, only under certain circumstances should a believer run around the church. Instances like when they were healed[35] or had repented, things like that. But my wife thought shouting every Sunday was just fine. She had lived that lifestyle from the time she could remember. I was Roman Catholic as a child and thought it best to sit still and be quiet in church. My present wife, however, thought all good Christians shouted and spoke in tongues. If they didn't, their salvation was doubtful.

However, after my present wife and I met, she stopped going to the prayer meetings and even shouted much less than before. She became very quiet. She later told me she had put me above God. I didn't understand that statement then, and I still don't. Nonetheless, I do understand her thought process better now than I did back then.

# An Honest Woman

After she came over a couple times, whenever I kissed her, she would groan and make all kinds of commotion. I thought she was about to orgasm while I kissed her. Within a few days, we were having full-blown sex. And let me tell you, it was more heavenly than I had ever dreamed possible. I kid you not; I recall reading articles in *Playboy* and *Penthouse* magazines when I was a teenager. I would think the stories were made up. Well, believe you me, my wife made the women in those articles seem like children's cartoon characters. I mean, those articles were for kids compared to what she did to me. I cannot express it in words! I was living on three to four hours of sleep per night. Seldom did she ever go home before two o'clock in the morning.

Sometimes she would say, "Let's go into the bedroom." This would scare me, because I knew I would have to get her out of the house before my son woke up. He was only eight, but he knew what adultery was and even told my pastor such. I denied it, of course. My first wife didn't even want sex. Her endocrine gland didn't work, so she didn't desire it. I was not going to pass up this opportunity. My plan was to make up for lost sex time, and let me tell you, we did!

I knew I wanted to marry her the moment I laid eyes on her, and she would tell me how God gave me to her. I've already mentioned she was the prettiest girl I had ever seen. Her face was angelic, with a voice to match. Her measurements were perfect. She would never tell me but my guess is they were 36, 22, 36. I think her dress size was a six or eight. She was tall and slender with blonde hair! She was fun to be with, and in bed, she would make every man's dream come true. I was in heaven. How could I not marry her? God had blessed me as He did Job. We both hit the bottom of the barrel only to rise to the top of the world. My dreams had come true, and I was going to make my new doll's dreams come true. (I called her doll or baby doll because she looked just like a Barbie doll.)

# The Wedding

I withdrew $25,000 from my 401k to pay off her charge card debt and to give her a very nice engagement ring, wedding, and honeymoon. The ring had a three-quarter-carat diamond. We rented a limo and a nice reception hall. Our wedding was very nice compared to her first marriage. She eloped the first time. I wanted to make her wedding special. She had a long, flowing, white dress. We went to Hawaii for our honeymoon. We gave her house trailer to her sons. She would live with me and my son in her new dream home.

# The Honeymoon

It was raining like crazy and windy as could be when we stepped foot in Hawaii. What a way to start out our honeymoon. A strange weather front had overtaken the islands, and the locals were all scurrying about in jackets and long pants. We didn't even get a lei when we got there. Finally, after alerting a taxi, we made it to the hotel. It was actually a condo on the ocean. I certainly didn't plan for my honey to view Hawaii this way. Last time I was there was with my first wife for our fifteenth wedding anniversary. It was a beautiful trip. This time, it would be 180 degrees different.

The next day, we went to the beach. My wife had her string bikini on but soon had to put on her wrap due to the wind blowing so badly. The sand was blowing so hard it stung our skin. After a short while, we went back to the condo. The following day, the wind began to die down so we took a walk on the beach. She again had on her bikini. In front of us was another girl, good looking but not as beautiful as my wife.

Without thinking I said, "Babe, that is the view every guy enjoys."

She didn't say anything, but later, I knew it bothered her. I had no idea at the time. My was wife was so pretty, and I thought confident of her beauty. I would constantly comment about her facial features, and how the rest of her body was perfect and fulfilling in every way. I would name her parts and talk about how wonderful she was. Along with that, and the confidence I thought she had, my comment about the bikini-clad woman ahead of us was only a fulfillment of her beauty and how I was the luckiest man in the world to have a girl like her. I had no idea she would look at my comment as if I wanted that girl ahead of us. That was the furthest thing from my mind. Granted, I would have never said such a thing to my first wife. We never talked about body parts, and she never initiated sex. She just put up with it. Therefore there would have been no reason for me to make such a comment. However, with my present wife, she would play with me even after I fell asleep. I would awake to this angel having sex with me. I just thought she was more confident than she was. Come to find out later, she actually had no self-confidence. In fact, if I didn't continuously tell her of her beauty, she would later think she was ugly. I had to keep her confidence up every hour of every day, or she would become depressed. I had no idea of this before we were married. I now fully realize why every couple should date for a year or so before marrying. But, I was an arrogant son of a gun and didn't need that kind of investigative experience before marrying my doll. Wow, was I in for a surprise!

# The Whale Episode

I wanted to give my new sweetie the best honeymoon ever, despite the terrible weather. After a couple of days, the weather did become more Hawaii-like, so I went to the hotel lobby to book a whale-watching dinner cruise. It would be a wonderful time, I thought. A nice dinner while the sun was setting over the ocean, with whales jumping about the ship—I figured she was sure to love it! However, in the process of booking the cruise, the ticket seller told me that the hors d'oeuvres cruise was much better. It was an open ship, and the whales could be seen better. She said the dinner cruise boat was closed in, and the whales were hard to see. When I asked about the dinner, she said it was very close to the dinner cruise. So, I booked the hors d'oeuvres cruise and couldn't wait to surprise my wife.

When we got to the boat dock, I was disappointed to see the cruise boat was very small with no place to sit down. The food was more like snacks and not at all like a dinner. But we did see plenty of whales, so the ticket seller was right in that respect. But I was very disappointed in that it was not comparable to a nice dinner cruise as I had intended. I told my wife we were going on a dinner cruise, and she had dressed very nice only to find everyone else in shorts and

T-shirts. The crew was friendly. There was a male captain and two young female shipmates. The latter would be my demise.

When we got back to the hotel, my wife was very depressed and looked disappointed. I apologized for the cruise not being what I had explained it would be. She said it wasn't that I didn't get a cruise with good food but rather that I wanted that cruise because it had prettier girls on it. I was confused. This was the first time in a long line of hundreds of episodes when she would accuse me of wanting pretty women. (And pretty women were always in eyeshot of wherever we happened to be.) I asked for an explanation. She said that I couldn't keep my eyes off the pretty shipmates. She wouldn't speak to me the rest of the evening. I was befuddled and more than a little disgruntled that my pretty doll would think such nonsense.

As time went on, however, I would find out how extremely different she was than the woman I had met three months earlier. Instead of a confident stalwart of a woman, she was a little girl who needed constant attention. The marriage that I thought would keep me stable would actually become very shaky. I thought that I, a man still grieving my first wife's death and in need of a mother for my eight-year-old son, had married a woman who would add strength to our family. But instead, I had to be the stalwart one, the one who would steer the ship and row the boat. I was already exhausted from forcing my son to accept my new wife as his stepmom. (Not in place of his mother in heaven but in addition to her. He didn't see it that way, and I would soon find out I would not only have to deal with him but also with my new wife's vulnerabilities.) She *needed* help when I thought she *was* help.

My marriage took a 180-degree turn. I had to be her knight, her prince, and her psychologist. My son, fortunately for me and for him, was a very strong-willed child. If it weren't for that, I don't know if I could have gotten him through his childhood years. My wife was no help; in fact, she was actually a detriment. In addition to my struggle to raise a child, I now had an adult child who needed even more attention than my son.

While in Hawaii, I called my son every day and made sure he talked to my wife. At this point, I was still confident she would be a benefit to him, and I knew I must be successful. He had to trust her as his stepmother (after his mom in heaven, who, I always assured him, was his real mom—albeit adoptive). Likewise, my new wife needed to trust him. (Years later, I found out my son had cried his little eyeballs out every day while I was gone. I wanted to honeymoon in Florida or the Bahamas for a few days, but she wanted a long one in Hawaii. Since she had nothing all of her life, I bit the bullet and forced myself to give her a dream honeymoon, even though it killed me to leave my boy for that long.)

One day we went to the Haleakala volcano in Maui. We got up at four o'clock in the morning to leave for the sunrise. My wife had a sore throat from the wind and rain days before, and on the way up, I began to experience a dizzy spell. I got these periodically after my first wife died. Once there, my wife was freezing because she hadn't brought the proper jacket. We couldn't wait to get back down and into our condo. (In contrast, when I went there with my first wife, not only was the weather perfect, but our trip to the volcano was too.) Needless to say, the dream honeymoon I wanted to give to my new wife was an absolute disaster. This would be an omen as to what our marriage would be.

The potential for a loving, trusting, wonderful relationship was out of reach. The potential for a perfect marriage was trashed due to circumstances surrounding us that we could not control. Even more, her misinterpretation of those circumstances caused her to consistently believe I did not love her. From then on, whenever things went wrong, it was because I had caused them. Whenever a pretty girl passed by, I wanted her. Her insecurity eventually became extreme paranoia.

# Trying to Make a Normal Life

My pastor had spoken of his family during multiple sermons over the years. His mother died during childbirth, but his sibling twins were healthy. Pastor was the same age when his mother died as my son was when my wife died. His dad remarried in less than a year. I also met my new wife in less than a year and married her just three months later. My pastor's father made his children call their stepmom Mom, basically because it was a good thing to do in order to keep the family as normal as possible. He had told his children their new stepmom was not to replace their mother in heaven, but she was their new mom on earth and would take good care of them. I did the same with my son. In fact, I was so intrigued with my pastor's admiration of his stepmom that I was confident my family would turn out the same. I asked him to be my best man and asked his father (whom I flew in from North Carolina and paid for all expenses) to perform the ceremony. I also asked advice from my new mentor, my pastor's father. Soon, however, I was to understand that my family was not like my pastor's. My wife was not like my pastor's mom.

The things that kept me motivated to make our family work were manifold. First, I had a strong Christian upbringing, and that was strengthened even more by my standing in our church at that time. I was the church librarian and a teacher. I was also a cofounder, along with my pastor, of our new School of Ministry, which would train new workers and preachers in the church and the surrounding area. I had studied the church extensively, along with its history and, of course, the Bible. My studies on divorce, remarriage, and the Christian family gave me confidence that no matter what happened, our family would be successful. Second, with all of the failures I thought I had made in my first marriage, God was now giving me a chance to make right in my second. Third, being the arrogant know-it-all that I was, there was no way I could get this wrong. "I will succeed," was my constant mind-set. Fourth, my wife's beauty and passion kept me bound in almost constant bliss.

I recall a TV show many years ago. In it, a pretty woman wanted constant sex with a guy, and he would often have to ward her off. That was me to a tee, except for the warding off. Our lovemaking was so intense sometimes that my son would knock on the bedroom door and ask if my wife was okay. He heard her screaming and thought something was wrong. Many a morning he would ask, "Daddy, why was Mommy screaming last night?" I would respond with something like, "She was sick, and her stomach hurt." Did I mention I was on cloud nine and a half in those days? Sure, she'd get mad at me during the day, but at night … look out!

# Everyday Life

Everyday living was much different after we were married. I had the most beautiful girl in the world living in my home. She adored me. My son, although he tolerated her, didn't particularly like her. He would cry his little eyes out at night, pleading for his mom in heaven. Whenever I woke up at night, I'd listen, and he'd often be crying. I'd go into his room and comfort him. It was a terrible time for him and me. But, as time went on, he grew more used to her and her quirks. (I would also ask my wife to go into his bedroom to comfort him, and she did. This was going to work, I just knew it!)

Often, in the evenings, the three of us would play board games. Whenever we did this, however, my wife was as competitive as my young son. I thought it strange she had to beat my son, as it was normal for me to let him win. In fact, there were times when she accused me of cheating to allow him to win the game. During those times, I would just wonder what was going on in her head. After a while, my son no longer wanted to play the games because he always lost to her. I would have to force him to play to keep the peace. Because of this, and things I have yet to say, I began to keep an eye on her, to ensure she wasn't too peculiar toward him in other things. She was.

One day, I was in the living room watching TV when I heard a commotion in the kitchen. It was my wife and son arguing. He was around nine years old. When I went into the kitchen, he looked up at me with his tear-filled puppy eyes and said, "Daddy, I don't know what to do." When I questioned them, she said she had told him to go into the garage and get seven bottles of water to put into the refrigerator. When my son opened the door, he noticed there were only a few bottles left in the container, so he brought the whole thing in. My wife, seeing nine bottles in the container, told him that she'd said seven bottles and that he needed to start listening to her. With that, they went back and forth about the schematics of seven bottles of water versus what was left in the package! I then told my son to go into the living room while I told my wife not to be so particular. Of course, she got mad at me for sticking up for my son and opposing her.

Such insignificant incidents that quickly turned into a disaster became the norm more and more as time went on. In fact, I don't know how many times I had to come home from work early or cut my class short to keep peace between the two of them and to decipher her misperception of reality.

# Trust

As I saw more of her mistrust in me and her competition with my son, I knew something wasn't right with her. I blamed her tormented past. I had already mentioned the fact she was raped and beaten as a child. She also told me her first marriage was a disaster because her husband cheated on her. Then, to add to her torment, her not-so-distant past was also terrible. She said she cried herself to sleep every night. She had no money. At one time, she was homeless and walked the streets of Detroit with two young boys without anyone to help her. Later, she moved from apartment to apartment because she couldn't afford the rent. She'd have to leave her sons home alone so she could work and put food on the table. This, I believe, is the reason she was so jealous of my son.

Her sons had nothing; my son had everything. Her sons had no father (that had anything to do with them); my son had a great father (yes, she even told me I was a great father). Her sons barely had a mother when they were young. She couldn't go to their ball games due to her work schedule. Now, she and I were going to all of my son's games. She was jealous, and I have to admit, with good reason. I would try to explain to her that her sons were now grown and on their own. They decided not to accept their dad's offer to send them to college after high school graduation. My son was still young, and we needed to raise him properly. Although she agreed, she didn't like it. I think she felt like she was betraying her own two boys. She had done nothing for them but did everything for my son. I'll have to admit, it had to be very hard.

# Girls

Much of this book has to do with women. Of all the problems we had, other women were by far the most challenging. In fact, probably 90 percent of our problems have to do with a woman who happened upon the scene, whether on TV, in a magazine, at the store, or while we were on vacation. She had many episodes concerning her perception of me and another woman.

One evening my son and I were watching a TV show called *Fear Factor*. On this weekly show, contestants would do crazy things to try and win a prize. This particular evening a young couple was standing at the edge of a pool in their bathing suits, waiting to dive in and perform their stunt. Just then, my wife walked into the room. She just stood there and stared at the TV and then at me. Finally, with a dirty look, she said, "I don't believe you are watching that!" I didn't understand at first, so I asked her what she meant. She explained that I was watching bikini girls on TV and a married man shouldn't be doing that. She then stormed down the hall and into the bedroom.

Because she was on her way out the door to her brand-new job, I was concerned. Not only was she working midnights for the first time, but she decided not to leave yet. And more importantly, I was befuddled that she was so mad about a TV show that my son, my first wife, and I had watched all the time. Finally, she came out of the bedroom with her hair redone and so much makeup she looked like a harlot. It scared me, to tell you the truth. Was she trying to tell me that if I can watch bikini girls, she can go looking for guys? I didn't know what to think. Without saying a word, she stormed out the door to work. Such incidents were becoming the norm approximately once every two weeks.

I can't remember what happened when she got home in the morning, but I do know what I did after such incidents for our first five years of marriage. I would look at her so lovingly and tenderly tell her I was very sorry. I would tell her that I hadn't meant to look at another woman. "You," I would say, "are the only girl for me." And then I would caress and stroke her hair. Sometimes this scene would last for fifteen minutes, sometimes for hours. But, it would almost always end in good sex. But that's not why I did it.

I knew she had a terrible past, and that past left some terrible scars. I was determined to erase those scars, even if it meant saying I was at fault. It was my honest opinion that in time she would finally see the light and realize what a good man I was and know she could trust me. These episodes did take a lot out of me, but I was determined to make it work. I was her savior, her knight in shining armor who would slay her dragons no matter the cost—unless that cost was my son. Later it looked like it could be just that; slowly, I came to the realization my plan would not work. For some reason, I set a time of five years at the maximum for her to see the light.

# The Password

One day when I got home from work, I was switching through the channels on the TV when a message popped on the screen that said, "Enter Password to Proceed." I thought this was odd, as I had watched this channel numerous times before. Then another channel had the same message, then another. I couldn't watch some of the channels without entering a password. I mentioned this to my son, and he said, "Yeah, Mom put a password on those channels." I asked him why, and he just said it was so we couldn't watch them. He didn't know the password either.

When my wife came home, I asked her about it. She said she didn't want us watching certain channels because they had scantily clad women on them and a young boy and a married man should not be watching such things. When I told her the channels she blocked were ones that played old TV shows and movies, she proceeded to tell me I shouldn't be watching *The Beverly Hillbillies* or *Top Gun*. This was a classic case of her paranoia concerning other women.

She understood the verse in the Bible concerning men looking at another woman with lust in their eyes[36] to an absolute and disproportionate extreme. The proper understanding of the verse concerned a man wanting to have sex with a woman who was not his wife. Jesus goes on to say that if the man desires her, he is as good as committing adultery. Jesus called this "committing adultery in his heart." In another scripture, Jesus makes a similar statement concerning murder. He says that if a man hates his brother, it is as good as committing murder in his heart.[37] This is the Christian message: having a desire to sin is sin already. If a person attempts murder but the person does not die, he has committed murder in his heart, although the law puts a limitation on this. Jesus goes further in that He says that even if we honestly desire it, our hearts are murderous. A Christian is to be pure and not wish these things. He is to love his neighbor, and only make love to his wife. His desire is for the benefit of his wife and fellow man. Christianity teaches that truth is in the heart of man, not only in his actions. What he wants to perform is what counts, even if he doesn't have the chance to act it out.

I couldn't explain my wife's actions at this point, as we hadn't been married for long yet, but I knew it wasn't normal. (Later, I would realize it was due to her inability to think in grey areas. To her, life was black or white. Actions were right or wrong, with nothing in between. There is no such thing as a fairly bad act, only terrible ones. A glance at a woman was as good as committing adultery.) One reason I was incapable of diagnosing what my wife was doing was due to the fact that I was still mourning my first wife's death and could not concentrate very well.

I mentioned my dizzy spells. These continued for a year or so into my second marriage. My present wife was, and is, a very religious person but not in the normal sense. What I mean is that although she was extremely religious, it was a type that looked at the actions of others and ensured they were doing right at the expense of her acting non-Christian in doing so. The password situation is a prime example. When *The Beverly Hillbillies* came on TV, the only thing she saw was a pretty blonde named Ellie Mae in short shorts and a low-cut top and her husband looking at that scene. In my wife's mind, the only reason I wanted to watch *The Beverly Hillbillies* was to lust after Ellie Mae. In so doing, I was committing adultery in my heart. Because there was no way a husband of hers was going to cheat on her, she was not going to allow me to watch the show. Therefore, she put the password on the TV for the good of me and my son.

If you are having trouble following this, just think about how I felt. Here was my beautiful wife, who was very jealous of other women, protecting my own Christianity, and I didn't even know what in the world she was trying to protect!

"Ellie Mae?!" I said. "Ellie Mae?! You are worried about me having lustful thoughts about Ellie Mae, so you password protected it so I couldn't watch it? To ensure I don't commit heart adultery, my wife has to protect me by blocking TV channels like TV Land?"

I blew up! I think that was the first time I ever yelled at her. She would not tell me the password. Finally, after making her understand very clearly that I would not put up with it, even if it meant throwing that TV away, cancelling our cable, and starting over with only my name and password on it, she finally gave in. She never did tell me the password. Rather, she took the password off all of the channels, even the ones that my son really should not have watched. Here's the black and white again. Instead of discussing it and deciding together what my son should watch and password accordingly or blocking the channels no one should watch and password protecting channels my son should not watch, she just took the password off of everything. Then she said something like, "Fine, sin, and let your son sin!"

# That Darn Pool

Every relationship has quirks. Ours wasn't unique in that respect, but the quirks we had were definitely unique. One evening, before we were married, I had a terrible dizzy spell. (By the way, I underwent extensive testing, but nothing was found. I am convinced they were caused by the terrible and constant mind-wrenching crying I had done continuously for the ten months from my wife's death till I met my present wife. I tried to stop the crying because I was afraid I might snap something in my head. But I couldn't. The spells would be triggered by getting too little sleep, drinking too much coffee, or concentrating too hard.)

During the midst of this particular spell, my parents came over to the house. My mom and sister were saints during this time. I could write a book on what they did for me during my terrible mourning before I remarried. When I called my girl and told her I had the spell but was feeling better, she said she'd be right there. I told her not to leave work because I was fine now, but she insisted. She was a nurse's assistant and worked at an assisted living home. As it was around nine o'clock at night, she still had two hours left of her shift. Instead of waiting till then, she called her boss and said I was sick and left the elderly alone. Her boss told her she must wait till someone relieved her, but my girl insisted I was more important. So, needless to say, her boss fired her.

Around nine thirty or so, she arrived at the house. She told my parents she would stay with me, so they went home. I wondered what my parents thought. My girl, whom I had only known for a few weeks, would stay with me? Did they know she planned on spending the night?

After they left, I put my son to bed. I told the woman who would later become my wife that the couch in the living room was comfortable if she wanted to spend the night. She said she was definitely not going to leave me alone. I was very uncomfortable with her staying, especially with my parents apparently knowing and my son there also. But who was I to tell a perfectly beautiful angel to get out of my house? So, she slept on the couch, and I went to my bed.

During the night, I couldn't sleep. It wasn't because I was dizzy, for that had passed. Only the normal aftermath resided, which was a numbing of my forehead. It was odd; whenever these spells occurred, my forehead always got numb. Anyway, it was around two o'clock in the morning when I got out of bed and put a towel wrap on. I walked into the living room where the angelic creature lay asleep. I knelt down by her head and pulled up my towel. To my absolute surprise, she grabbed me and put it all the way down her throat! I released in her, and she swallowed. I then went back to bed surprised and delighted, to say the least.

In the morning, I took my boy to school, and she either went home or to her cleaning job, I can't remember which. That evening when she came over, I asked her how her day was. She said she was so full of energy that day that it must have been my semen that gave it to her! Oh my God! Oh my God! Oh my God! I was so … so … so … I don't know. I just knew this was an angel God had sent down from heaven to take me from my constant and torturous pain. God had saved me on earth and had given me a large piece of heaven. He was good, and my wife in heaven was in agreement.

I had always understood that once people go to heaven, they are pure and holy. This means that any wrong people had done them while on earth was forgiven. Jesus forgave His murderers and told us to do the same. Once in heaven, we would only want blessings on all of our loved ones. Therefore, I understood my wife had forgiven me for all the wrong things I had done (which, in fact, were not bad, just normal things husbands and wives do, silly arguments and such). Did she ask the Lord to give me a sexy wife because she didn't give me such things due to her hormone deficiencies? I wondered if this was the case. Either way, I thanked God. But, this new angelic creature and I weren't married yet! Wait a minute!

As is usually the case, when people do things they want to do but really should not be doing, they rationalize. I was the master of rationalization but didn't realize it. In so doing, I told my future wife that I would soon marry her, but I couldn't give her an engagement ring yet because it would be too hard on my son and family, not to mention my deceased wife's parents. But, I promised, it would be soon (and, in fact, it was).

I told her the story of Isaac and Rebecca. I was Isaac, I told her, and she was Rebecca.[38] As the story goes, when Abraham realized his son was of age, he sent his servant to find Isaac a wife. He needed to carry on the lineage that

God had promised him. His servant did, and when Isaac saw her, he invited her into his tent, and they consummated their marriage without ceremony first. I told my girl we had consummated our marriage, and were continuing to do so, before our marriage ceremony. We were as good as married in God's eyes; therefore, we needn't worry. She didn't buy it but still continued to invite me to my bed with her till we did perform the ceremony a couple of months later.

But why did she quit her job to stay with me that night? My thoughts went in two directions. First, she must really love me to be so concerned as to quit her job to be with me during my spell. And second, that was really stupid. Because my dizziness had passed and my parents were there, there was no need. (Yes, a man in his late forties had to have his parents there. But they knew how helpless I had been since my wife died.) I just wondered what her mind was like to think that way. But, her stay there made me forget any silliness on her part. It was as if a kid was told there were chocolate chip cookies in the jar, but he must wait till after dinner. What harm was it to just eat one before dinner? Certainly, if he keeps it a secret from everyone, God would overlook such an act, especially if he was starving and the cookie kept shouting through the jar, "Eat me, eat me! You must eat me, or I'll die!" What would the boy do? Why, he would eat the cookie to put it out of its misery and to satisfy his cravings. It was a no-brainer. Everybody was happy. Problem was, my cookie had second thoughts.

It was after we had had intercourse that my girl told me she couldn't come over one night. She came over every night prior and stayed till after midnight. What was different about this evening? When I pressed her, she said she had to clean her house. I said, "I have an answer for that. My son and I will grab some supper and bring it over to your place, and then we'll help you clean." Because she couldn't give me a definite no, that's what I did. When we got there, she did a couple of things around her place while my son and I ate. Afterward, we just sat and talked. She didn't have to clean her house! But I didn't press her.

Because by the next evening we were back to normal, I kind of forgot about it. After we were married, she told me why she didn't come over that evening. She was going to break it off with me. Why? Because we'd had sex, and having sex before marriage was wrong, so she was going to break up with me. I was baffled by her logic. My logic dictates that if a man and woman have intercourse, they should get married, not break up. They consummated their relationship, and in God's eyes, they were actually married before the contract was signed rather than afterward. Adultery is committing sex outside of marriage or before marriage, but if the contract is signed after consummation (as long as there is no other marriage and no other relationship going on—and no illegitimate divorce or separation, etc.), all is well and good. The sin of sex before marriage is erased. The couple did the right thing.

This is very similar (although it may not be identical) to the old way of looking at things. In the old days, if a man got a girl pregnant, he married her. It was plain and simple. Also, in many a case, if a father found out his daughter had sex with a man, as long as he was a good man, the father would desire or, shall I say, demand that he make an honest woman out of her, especially if family, friends, and acquaintances were aware of it. That was my thinking, right or wrong. I am not so sure of that line of logic now, but back then, before my present wife "done me wrong," it was. If I knew then that my wife would desert me now, I don't know if I would have married her (my head was spinning so fast I couldn't think straight). But I had no idea back then that she would desert me now. I did not know she was a runner. In those days, I would never have believed she would do what she has done to me today. However, I should have tried to figure out why she did not want to see me after we'd had sex the evening(s) before. For someone in his right mind, that would have been a red flag. But I only saw an angel of light who saved me from the darkness of hell on earth. I couldn't help it. How could God torment me a second time? That was impossible, I thought.

Another red flag that popped its ugly head occurred just a couple of months after we were married. We were married in March. It was in May when my wife began to complain that her legs were hurting. She also complained much about the fumes from cleaners she used in housecleaning. When we met, she worked two jobs. After she quit the nursing home, she only cleaned houses three days per week, four hours each day. I told her she didn't have to work, so she quit. A week or two later, she had a big smile on her face when I came home from work. She said she found a swimming pool for five thousand dollars. She said it would be good for her legs. It was a large above-ground pool that her friend had found. The seller said he'd disassemble and then reassemble it at our house for free. We really didn't have a very good place for a pool, as our back yard was full of trees and butted up to a woods. In fact, I'd had a pool for my son a couple of years prior, and the water never got warm enough to swim in. The kids would hop out of the pool every time the air conditioner kicked on to warm themselves with the warm air blowing from the condenser. I can still see their shivers large as fish jumping out of the water. Anyway, we looked at the pool in question and told the people we'd take it. I told her I'd add a heater and, of course, chop down some trees.

The next day, the pool people called and said they had changed their minds; their kids had talked them out of selling the pool. My wife was very disappointed and said her hurting legs really needed that pool. So, we began to search for a new one. In the meantime, she saw doctors and a neurologist to try and figure out what was wrong with her legs. Every doctor and every test stated that there was nothing wrong. In fact, I recall the expression on the neurologist's face when he said to her, "There is nothing wrong with your legs." Of course, this upset me a bit since, at this early point in our marriage, I only wanted my doll to be healthy and did not believe she would make up such a story so she could quit work and get a swimming pool. However, now I know better.

Our hunt for a swimming pool proceeded from this used five thousand-dollar pool to an equivalent twelve thousand-dollar pool with a heater to a semiabove-ground pool with a deck for sixteen thousand dollars, to a prefab built-in pool for twenty thousand dollars, to the pool we finally bought. It was a kidney-shaped built-in pool with a price tag of thirty-five thousand dollars. To say the least, I was more than a little nervous about spending so much money. Our present bills took care of my paycheck, and I had already stopped saving for my son's education when we were married due to trying to line out my finances and regrouping. We had a mortgage, a motorcycle, and two car payments. However, my doll wanted a pool. But how could I afford it? (Believe it or not, I was also a little concerned she may leave me if I didn't get her the pool. Her episodes put me on edge, and I didn't know which way to turn many times.)

I had an idea. I would remortgage my home. The house we lived in was worth approximately $215,000, but I only owed $90,000. Therefore, in line with my misguided thinking since my wife's death a little more than a year before, I decided to consolidate our loans into this new mortgage along with our new pool. My job was secure, and I would have it paid off by the time I retired. Concerning my son's education, I figured if worse came to worst, I'd use part of my 401k to pay for it. (Another sore point with my wife was saving for my son's education when her sons had nothing in that respect. Sure, they were in their midtwenties, but my wife treated them like little kids.) By the end of summer, the pool was in. Miraculously, even before she jumped into the pool the first time, her legs stopped hurting. How that happened, I didn't know, but at that point in our marriage, I didn't care. I was only glad her legs quit hurting and my doll was happy.

My wife's friend did give her a piece of her mind, though. She told my wife she was taking advantage of me. My wife immediately became her enemy. The woman had been one of her bridesmaids just a few months earlier and her very good friend for years. I did agree that my wife was taking advantage of my good nature, expecting me to refinance my home in order to get her a new swimming pool, but that was my business. Besides, I didn't want anyone to think my wife was taking advantage of me, although it was true. (I have been having thoughts of calling this woman to tell her she was right after all, since she and my wife are not talking anyway and I am getting a divorce. But, I don't know what good that would do anyone.)

# The Family Reunion

My wife has a large family. She is one of eleven brothers and sisters. It's a very close-knit family, but at the same time, very dysfunctional. Her mom had been married five times but, before she died, was single. (Note, however, that all of her children were from her first marriage.) She was the widow of two husbands but had divorced the other three. (I understand she divorced the last one because he urinated in the toilet without lifting the seat and didn't let her watch her TV stations when he wanted to watch something.)

My wife's oldest sister had been married twice, but her present marriage is happy. In fact, my wife considers her and her present husband the ideal couple. They are, in fact, very nice people and do appear to be very much in love. Her other brothers and sisters are quite different, however. Two of the sisters had never been married but had had multiple live-in boyfriends. The one, whom my wife constantly holds on a pedestal because of her beauty (even though she is not as pretty as my wife), often visited other male acquaintances while living with another.

My wife's family is as promiscuous as they come. Her other sisters are less promiscuous but still have had multiple husbands or boyfriends. Her brothers are no better. One, who is also a preacher, was on wife number five when I met him. Two of his previous wives had sex with his (and my wife's) stepfather, or so my wife tells the story. He therefore had good cause to divorce them. (Actually, as I write this, he is now on wife number six.) Her other brothers are more conservative, with only two to four wives each (sequentially, of course).

Every year, the family used to gather at their mother's house. It was a very good time the first day or so. I enjoyed listening to each of them trying to outdo the others. With their vacations, careers, cars, and houses, most were well off. I always felt sorry for my wife's past as they chatted, realizing that before she met me, she could only listen to these conversations. She was always the underdog with two sons, no husband, and no money. Well, by golly, now she had a husband and money too; she was now enjoying the camaraderie. She also lived in a nice house, drove a nice car, and took good vacations. But this fun for my wife and I would be cut short by the second day.

The expression on her face would begin to change to a frown. Every reunion was the same. She would accuse me of wanting her sister (the pretty one with many boyfriends). Then, from that day forward, our good time at the reunion was ruined. She claimed this sister had sex with her ex-husband multiple times, and she accused me of wanting to do the same. At future reunions, I would make it a point to never talk to that sister and not look at her unless I absolutely had to due to her asking a question or something. After three or four of these reunions, I told my wife I was through. I would go to no more, and I did not.

# Vacations and Not

My first wife and I used to go on a nice vacation every two or three years. The years in between we'd go on a low-expense trip. It would be somewhere cheap and close. This made our nice vacations special and also saved us a lot of money. Speaking of saving money, when we did take a nice vacation, we'd get the less expensive hotel away from the beach. Sometimes we'd splurge, but conservatively. In other words, we didn't go overboard or vacation above our means. It was different with my present wife.

When my present wife and I went on vacation, it was always on the ocean and in a suite. No price was too high. We did this at least once per year. Every year our nice vacation was in addition to a short vacation for just me and her. For these, we'd leave my son at his grandparents, while we went out of town alone.

One time early in our marriage, my wife wanted to go to the King's Island Amusement Park for the weekend in Cincinnati, Ohio. I told her that would be great and our son would love it. She looked at me puzzled and said, "No, just you and me." Now I was puzzled. The point was, she wanted us to go on a boyfriend/girlfriend date. She had never done anything like that and wanted us to do it—two middle-aged people on a boyfriend/girlfriend date. We went on a date every Saturday night, but this would be special. So, more than a little embarrassed, I told my son and his grandparents we were going to Saginaw, Michigan, for a minivacation, just me and my doll. My son had no clue what was in Saginaw, so he didn't think twice. His grandparents didn't ask questions.

During the course of my first marriage, I grew to love my wife's parents more and more. They were the nicest people you'd ever want to meet. When my son was born, he grew so attached to them that after his mom died, they were not just good family, but his best friends. Therefore, after meeting my present wife, I didn't have the heart to pull him from them, so they continued to be a part of our lives. They accepted my wife with loving arms, something I don't know if I could have done. In fact, when their other grandson (my nephew and my son's cousin)[39] was married, everyone insisted my present wife be a part of the family wedding pictures. That family is the greatest. They were a big part in my son's happiness as a child. They are gone now, but he was able to enjoy them till his teen years. He still misses them. I do too.

So, we went to King's Island and had a good time. I was certainly uncomfortable, though, wishing my son was with us like in normal families. Our family vacations were different, however. I don't mean so much the fact that my son would be with us but that other women would put a damper on them. Yes, the women. Believe it or not, there are always women when on vacation—at the beach, on the street, and in restaurants! We were at a restaurant in Mackinaw City, Michigan, one summer. While waiting for the light show to begin, my son wanted something to eat. So, he and I went to the stand and purchased our food but then saw a much nicer spot to sit. It was on the other side of the patio. So I sat my food on the table and went to tell my wife. While the three of us were eating at this new table, I noticed my wife's expression change. (I was beginning to recognize the change in her facial expression when an episode was about to occur.) We ate and then watched the light show.

When we returned to our hotel, she wouldn't speak to me. The following morning I asked what was wrong. She said that the only reason I wanted to move to that table was so I'd be closer to the pretty women a few tables over. I told her I didn't even know there were women there. Needless to say, the rest of our vacation was ruined. This time, though, I'd had it. I told the family we were going home early. My son, however, began to beg me in tears not to leave, so I decided to tough it out. From that point forward, it was a miserable trip for me.

Another time we were on our way to Minneapolis, Minnesota, and stopped at a hotel in the evening part way there. We had two double beds in the room, one for my wife and me and one a few feet away for my son. After we had turned the lights off and went to bed, my wife was more than a little frisky. I was nervous, not only because my son was just a few feet away and facing us, asleep, but because the parking lot lights shined through the window curtains so it wasn't very dark in our room. I could see my son very clearly. He was certainly asleep but might wake with any noise. My wife soon turned her back to me and put me inside her. Since I didn't want to wake my son, I didn't move a lot and ensured I was quiet. After a bit, I finished by business and then relaxed.

The next morning, my wife wouldn't speak to me. I asked what was wrong, but she wouldn't say. As we proceeded onto the highway and toward Minneapolis, I could see she was mad as a hornet. We continued in silence the rest of the way there. Once at the hotel, I asked her very clearly what the problem was. She still would not answer. The following morning, I told her if she didn't lighten up, we'd go home immediately.

She said, "How would you like to be horny all day long and not be able to do anything about it?"

I said, "What?"

She explained that when she put me inside of her the night before she wanted to orgasm, but after I did my thing, I went to sleep. I asked her how I was supposed to know that. I was trying to be quiet, and if I tried to make her orgasm, I'd be making enough noise to wake up my son, not to mention the noise she would have made. I told her she should have let me know that. She then proceeded to tell me how happy she was to be going on vacation with me, and that's why she was so horny that night. But because I didn't release her, she was pent up, horny, and miserable the whole next day! Oh my God, I had a sex monster on my hands! But I had already known that. The rest of the trip turned out to be pretty good, however, except for a few bumps, mostly between her and my son.

Whenever we took a trip, I wanted to let my son bring a buddy, but she didn't want him to. She said it was too much hassle having to watch his friend also, so most of the time it was just the three of us. Problems would often arise, however, when my son wanted to do kid things and my wife adult things. She would never budge, so he'd end up doing stuff alone, or I would go with him and she'd be mad because I left her alone.

At Disney World, he went off on his own (this was when he was old enough to do so). We told him to meet up with us at a certain time and place. I also kept tabs via text or cell phone. He was fine with it and quickly made friends to hang with during the day. The same occurred at other amusement parks. We'd walk around, while my son rode the rides. We'd ride too, but often, my wife and son wanted different rides. I'd try my best to keep us together, and sometimes I did. As often as I could, I'd have my wife wait on the bench while my son and I went on a ride. Or, my wife and I'd wait while he rode. But often, he'd just take off on his own. I didn't like that but tried very hard to keep the peace without forfeiting my son's enjoyment during vacation. Because of this, she'd complain I loved my son more than I loved her.

Speaking of amusement parks, one time while on our way to the hotel near Cedar Point, my wife and I noticed a lingerie shop. She always wore sexy clothing. She wore thongs and sheer bras, which drove me crazy. At night, she wore a very short and skimpy nightie, if anything at all. Well, once we got to the hotel, I told her I'd like to go back to that lingerie shop and get her a nice nightie. She said she'd rather go, so I told her to spend what she wanted, and I'd see her when she got back. To my delight and surprise, when she opened the bag, it wasn't lingerie at all. It was $240 worth of sex toys! Oh my God, oh my God, oh my God! Will heaven ever stop getting better? There were dildos, vaginas, nipple vibrators, sex positions graphically displayed in a book, and

I can't remember what all. She said she was so horny in the shop while looking at all the pictures and talking to the lady there, she couldn't stop buying stuff. I told her it was just fine with me. Needless to say, we had many evenings of fun with that bag of toys.

Another time, while at an amusement park, we were eating breakfast at the hotel buffet. While sitting across from her, I noticed some slight features that resembled her mother. The way the light was shining on her face made me notice. Since I had realized early on that compliments to her earned me favors in the evening, I thought I'd give her one. I said, "The way the light is shining on your face kind of reminds me of your mother a little bit." Her face quickly changed to a frown; she got up and went to the hotel room. My son and I just looked at each other in amazement and wonder. She was always talking about how beautiful her mother was, and I figured such a comment would bring joy to her. However, the only thing that came to her mind when I said the word *mother* was old age and wrinkles. When my son and I went back to the hotel room, she refused to go to the park. She said she'd stay in the hotel room that day.

My son and I went to the park but returned to the hotel early that afternoon, hoping she'd have a change of heart. She wasn't in the room but rather lying on the edge of the pool in her string bikini. While scanning the pool area, I noted many guys taking their eyes off of her just as my eyes met theirs. (Sometimes I made a game of it. Whenever we were out in public, the guys would stare at her. I'd guess to myself how many guys I could stare down that day. Guys will always take their eyes off of the girl, once her man looks at them. At least that's been my experience.) I told her to come to the park with us, but she was mad and never did go to the park.

Another time, we were at a water park. Again, my wife was in her bikini. While sitting at the wave pool, my son came out of the water saying he was hungry. I asked my wife if she was hungry, but she was not and wanted to stay while we went to find something to eat. We went to the stand just a stone's throw from the pool and sat down and ate hot dogs and fries. When finished, we got up and began to return to the pool only to find my wife coming our way. She was mad as a hornet again and accused me of only wanting to get a bite to eat so I could look at all the pretty women in bikinis! I told her she was prettier than any of them, and I just wanted a hot dog. She didn't buy it. Another vacation was ruined. I could give example after example and vacation after vacation that were ruined because my wife thought I wanted to look at women other than her. The situation was kind of like a Cadillac being jealous of an old, beat-up Chevy. Why would I even have the energy to want other women when the prettiest girl in the world wore me out every night?

# Working from Home

During the first couple of years of our marriage, I had the opportunity to work from home on Mondays. This meant I didn't have to get ready for work in the morning and make the forty-five-minute drive. Before I married my present wife, it was a great way to get work done from the comfort of my own home. However, after I married, the situation changed drastically. Not only did I not get ready for work, I hardly even got out of bed!

After sending my son off to school, I'd return to bed and have sex till the early afternoon. One day I counted my wife having nine orgasms! Yes, nine. I counted them. She'd hardly rest between them before we'd go at it again. The last couple, I will admit, she did beg me to stop, but I told her one more, then one more. Oh my God, oh my God, oh my God! My wife was a horny wild woman. I was in seventh heaven. Can you blame me for giving her anything she wanted, whether pool, vacation, or Lexus?

It didn't matter where we were at, she'd want to go at it. We did it in the pool and in the hot tub. One day, I was sitting on our deck in the backyard. She came up to me all sexy after coming out of the pool. She took off her bikini and pulled my pants down to my knees. She then climbed on top of me, and, well, you know the rest. I kept looking around to make sure no one was approaching around the corner of the house. Then I'd glance in the windows to make sure my son wasn't around. To say the least, although nervous as could be, I was having the time of my life. Finally, she put her bikini back on and went into the house.

She lived in a black-and-white world. Either things were good, or they were bad. They were black, or they were white. It was this or that, never the other. I don't recall what else happened that day, but I do know she left my head spinning. Also, it wouldn't surprise me if she got upset later due to a pretty woman flashing across the screen of the TV set during an advertisement. Why would that concern her? Why, because I would want that woman more than I wanted her that afternoon on the deck. Her insecurities were extreme, and so were her moods and her actions.

# Twenty-Four Hours

One day she had another episode. I don't recall what caused it, but she left abruptly in her car without saying a word. During the following hours, I called and texted her, but she didn't reply. I called her sons to contact her, but they said they couldn't make contact either. She had done such things in the past, but she would always come home by midnight or so. She'd get mad at me about something, almost always due to a woman, and then just leave and not answer my calls until hours later. When she didn't leave in her car, she'd lock herself in the bathroom. Because I would be concerned for her well-being, I would often force the door open to make sure she hadn't swallowed a bottle of pills. Then I would sit on the floor with her, stroke her hair, and tell her how much I loved her. Often this would take care of things, but sometimes she'd fly out the door and take off in the car anyway. If it was a situation I thought she may get into an accident due to her being so upset, I'd disconnect the sparkplug wires before she had a chance to drive away. I don't know how many times she did this, but it had to be dozens, no, many dozens of times.

This particular time, however, she didn't come home by midnight or shortly thereafter. I woke up the following morning (by the way, I am now reminded of all the times I got no sleep at night due to her and her odd tactics), and she was still gone. I called her friends, but no one knew where she was. Finally, in the afternoon, she came home. She came up to me, crying and said, "I am so sorry, I am so sorry." This was the first and only time she ever told me she was sorry. I asked where she had been, and she said at a hotel, alone, in town. In those days, I didn't ask a lot of questions, not because I was afraid of her response but because I knew I could trust her in such instances. In other words, her being with another man was the furthest thing from my mind. I was convinced she was true to me in that respect. In fact, as I write this paragraph, I am convinced of that, and I am only a month away from our divorce trial date. To this day, I think she was just so upset that she got a hotel room. Although, and you will think I am crazy, sometimes she left saying, "I'm going to find someone who will love me." That's the way she was. She constantly thought I did not love her. I had to tell her all the time. And when I commended my son on something, which I did often, I had to make sure I did the same for her.

# Her Odd Dreams

Another thing that puzzled me about my wife, from the early days of our marriage to the day she left me the first time, were her many dreams. Even more puzzling was the fact that she didn't mind telling me about them. As time went on, she even enjoyed telling me. I would wonder about these dreams and her telling me about them, but at the same time, I had full trust in her that she would not act them out. She'd say she didn't know why she dreamed them. But I would tell her she couldn't help what she dreamt. Nonetheless, as mentioned already, at times she appeared to enjoy telling me. I don't know if she was trying to make me jealous or what it was, but I was never jealous.

When I married her, although not in my right mind about many things, I could think clearly concerning some things. One was that I would continue to do an excellent job raising my boy. God gave him to me, and I would not shirk that responsibility. The other was I would not be jealous of my wife. Her beauty could certainly cause reason for jealously, but I knew very well that if I let one shade of jealousy come into our marriage, it would destroy me. To this day, I have not let jealousy in. With her, however, it was a drastically different story, and her jealously is what eventually destroyed our marriage.

The first of these many occurrences happened early in our marriage. My wife woke up and told me she'd had a terrible dream. With just a little prodding, she told me she was with her old boyfriend in this dream. (Now, her old boyfriend was about ten years younger than her. She had broken up with him only months before we met. She told me that the reason for the breakup was because our pastor told him to break it off. She said they never had sex; in fact, they never even kissed. The pastor said she would be trouble for him, and it was in his best interest. I just wrote this off and didn't think much more about it. However, after further pondering, I had begun to realize that the woman I had married was the very woman whom my wife told me to stay away from because she was a troublemaker. Wow, my first wife warned me of my trouble to come. I am amazed.) Anyway, she said in the dream with her boyfriend they were both naked in bed and having sex. She said she didn't try to fight him off but wanted to have sex with him. To say the least, I was dumbfounded, but with everything else she said and was doing, then and in the future, this really was nothing for me to worry too much about.

Another morning she woke up and told me she had just had a nightmare. Guys were chasing her and were trying to have sex with her. She woke up before they caught her. Another time she dreamed a couple of guys were raping her, but I was too busy talking to her sister (the one she consistently accused me of wanting to have sex with). She told me she couldn't believe I wouldn't help her. She acted as if it were my fault I didn't help her in her dream!

Another time she said she caught me having sex with her sister in a dream. Her dreams continued approximately once per week. There were many dozens of them. I just wrote them off as dreams of a sex maniac, as that is what she was. However, the last one I remember her telling me about was a very dramatic one, and when she told me, she acted as if she had really enjoyed this dream. She was in a building, and guys were chasing her. They wanted to have sex with her. She said there were about a half dozen guys, and they were all naked. They were tall, dark, handsome, and very muscular. Their penises were very large, and they were erect. She made it a point to tell me a second time that these guys were very handsome and had large, erect penises.

This was the first time she seemed to really enjoy telling me about her dream. And her emphasizing the sexual characteristics of the men in her dream more than once was something new and different. This dream was one of the last or possibly the last dream she told me about. It was after I began to get mad at her for falsely accusing me of wanting other women. It was a few years ago and before she left me the first time. I don't recall her telling me about any dreams since then.

Why didn't I think she may act these dreams out? She had plenty of opportunities. After all, I did mention she left me for twenty-four hours one time. She also left many evenings, not returning till midnight or so. I know you, the reader, are thinking these are red flags, but I know why she left. She had to flee when situations became uncomfortable. When we had a disagreement, she'd go for a drive. Sometimes, while on these drives, she'd get into an accident. She'd lose concentration or black out and then lose control of her car.

(She would back up without looking and once backed into my lawn tractor. Sometimes she would run into cars in parking lots. Once, she ran head on into a truck and was hospitalized for a weekend.) Often, when she left in her fit of rage, she'd say she would find someone who would love her. But again, I just considered these words of jealously. The only instances of sex outside of our relationship were before we met. In fact, there were two separate sets of incidents that I am aware of.

First of all, she wasn't a bit ashamed of talking of previous dates and boyfriends. In every instance but one, she'd always say the guy was out for only one thing, so she'd break it off. However, even though many had tried, only one of these beaus succeeded. He was a widower. I knew his wife before she died, as she had gone to our church, but I had never met him. She was quite a bit younger than me, so this guy was probably younger than my wife. My wife did date a number of men younger than her. After all, she looked twenty years younger than she actually was. Anyway, she said she spent the night with him, and they had sex. They both wanted it, and she enjoyed it. She told me of this before we were married but after we had sex for the first time. Actually, our first time was oral. I moved down on her while she put me all the way down her throat. She swallowed my semen just before she orgasmed. After we were done, she said with a big smile on her face, "I needed that." *Wow*, I thought, *so did I.* I had never had a woman give me oral sex before. When I told her, she didn't believe me (The incident after my dizzy spell, mentioned earlier, was the second.)

The other occurrence was not with a boyfriend but with her ex-husband. She said that for years after her divorce, when her husband came over to visit the boys, later that evening he would go into the bedroom and drop his pants. They would then have sex. They had sex many times and for quite some time after their divorce. But, she said it had been many years before we met. Although unconsciously, this is probably a big reason why I told her I didn't want her visiting her former in-laws. I thought, if she did, there was a chance she may meet her ex. In hindsight, I wish I would not have said that.

In those days, she didn't argue (she just got mad and locked herself in a room or took off in the car). But much later, she told me I should have let her visit them for her sons' sake. I had never thought of it that way. I should have, but I did not. If she had tried to reason with me instead of just believing one thing without argument, she probably would have convinced me to let her visit them. But since she never brought it up and she never gave me evidence she may have wanted to, I just figured she fully agreed. Now, many years later, I know she really wanted to visit some of her former in-laws with her sons. After all, they were their aunts, uncles, and cousins, just as my son had the same on my first wife's side. But, she kept it bottled up inside. Her black-or-white, yes-or-no, right-or-wrong mentality would not let her do otherwise.

## Walking on Eggshells

After six or so years of walking on eggshells and not knowing what her present mood was or how she would respond to anything I did or said, I'd finally had enough. I figured after almost six years of proving to her my love, but her still not knowing who I really was, was long enough. It was obvious my tactic was not working. I was very discouraged that I couldn't convince her of my unconditional love and devotion to her. I thought for sure that as she saw my life and how much I showed my love to her, she would come around and start trusting me. But it did not happen. (It is also amazing that I kept our problems hidden from everyone. No one had a clue we were having any issues until many years later. In fact, I would mention our love in my monthly news articles in our church paper. On that note, whenever I mentioned my son, I had to mention her; otherwise, she'd get mad. One time I wrote she was the most beautiful girl in the western hemisphere. Her response was, "Oh, I'm not the prettiest girl in the world?" She was excessively narcissistic.)

In fact, after so many years of being stabbed in the back while riding away on my white horse with her behind me after saving her from the dragon, I sometimes began to doubt my own sanity. I would think, *Am I not understanding the situation properly? Is she really the only one who doesn't get it, or am I also not presenting myself properly? Is she really the one who sees truth, and I am the psychotic?* These were questions that were beginning to roll through my mind.

At one point, I thought I really may be going crazy. I had to do something. I knew she was the one who needed help, but how could I convince her to get it? I knew if I just came out and told her she needed to see a psychiatrist (at this time I didn't know the difference between a psychiatrist and a psychologist), she would automatically think I believed she was crazy. That would be a mistake. Who knows what she would do in such a case. I needed to figure out what to do, and fast. If I didn't, I would go crazy and lose my mind, my son would become emotionally scarred for life, or who knows what else may happen.

I was beginning to have one-on-one talks with my son concerning his second mom. I would have to tell him not to worry, that I was in control, and I would be certain that Mom would not punish him without cause. In addition, I had to tell him very clearly that he would continue in sports. Because she continuously downplayed sports and hated to go to his games, he was beginning to give up. In fact, at one point he told me he was quitting them. This blew me away, because sports were his life. I had also noticed he was no longer the star player on his basketball and baseball teams like he used to be. But after a couple of hard talks, he began to get back on track. His faltering grades also began to come back into line. For the record, he did get back on track in all, including emotionally.

I knew there was no possible way God wanted me to continue as things were. I just knew I would eventually figure out what to do. But to this day, I am not sure if the path I took was the correct one.

I think I could have handled it better. I know I could have, but for the life of me, I still don't know what I could have done differently. What I did caused a downward spiral that has culminated into my present predicament. Nonetheless, and although I still am not convinced, everyone says it is for my own good. My attorneys, both pastors, my son, all my friends, and all of my family told me I needed to get rid of her. But I didn't want to. I wanted her to understand the reality that I loved her more than anything in the world.

# Sex, Preachers, and Hormones

Not too many years after we were married, my wife began to experience perimenopause. She was then in her midforties. It was time. During this period, she also said she began to experience less satisfaction during sex. She didn't seem to orgasm as much. This was a great concern for her. And, for that matter, it was for me too. I loved to hear her scream. I loved her to take it to the limit, so to speak. So, she began seeing her doctor who prescribed certain hormones. She also bought a book by Susan Somers called *The Sexy Years*.[40]

One day, she brought the book to me and showed me a certain paragraph. It said that if a woman wants to have better sex, she and her partner should rent porn movies together or visit Internet porn sites. She said it would spice up their sex life and should help the woman experience better sex. I looked at her and said, "Do you want to do that?" She said yes. So we went to the computer. She sat on the chair and searched the sites while I watched. As the movie clips played, she'd play with me. We did this for a few months. Then one day while at the video store, she asked if I wanted to go into the adult section. So, we went in.

She said, "Pick out a couple of movies, and we'll take them home and watch them."

She got no argument from me. So I picked out one and said, "Let's go." She told me to pick out another one, but I told her one should be plenty, as I was more than a little nervous poking around the adult section of the video store. So, we rented it and put it into the player on our bedroom TV. After watching about ten minutes of the movie, while we were having sex, she began to sob uncontrollably. I didn't know what to think, so I shut it off and asked what was wrong.

She said, "You are pretending you are having sex with the girl on the screen while having sex with me!" All the while, she was sobbing.

This broke my heart and made me mad at the same time. Nonetheless, this episode made me realize the porn stuff was not working. We never rented another porn movie or watched porn on the Internet again. Eventually, however, her sex drive did come back.

Due to the hormones she was on for menopause, Wellbutrin for depression, and periodically starting and stopping both whenever she felt like it, I decided to visit her doctors. Her emotions were all over the place, partially at least, due to her taking the medications whenever she felt like it instead of when her doctors told her to. My wife's hormone doctor told me if she did not take the hormones as she prescribed, they would cause her to be misguided psychologically. When I talked to our family doctor, who prescribed her Wellbutrin, he said she needed to take the dosage consistently. In a nutshell, it was my belief that the hormone pills, depression drugs, and menopause were causing my wife to act even worse than she had in the past.

We needed a doctor to keep everything in line and in perspective. Different doctors prescribing different drugs was not good. In fact, she was beginning to hallucinate, and her paranoia was increasing. She told me I had cameras in the house and was watching her every move. She said she saw a camera on the rearview mirror in the car and one inside the TV set. When I asked her to show me these cameras, she said I had taken them out the day before. Incidents such as this and much worse were becoming more and more common.

Then one day, while I was on my computer, my wireless NIC (network interface card) quit working. So I opened the network and print sharing utility to see what the problem was. She came into the den and looked at my screen. Immediately, she insisted I was setting my system up to remote into her computer without her knowing it so I could spy on what she was doing. I tried to explain to her I was only fixing my NIC, but she insisted I was setting up spy software. She asked me to show her certain menu items so she could prove I was a covert spy. I did humor her for a bit, but after a while, I became irritated with her nonsense and told her I was going to reboot for the changes to take effect. When the system came back up, she wanted to see another item. When it didn't display like she thought it should, she said I reset it with the reboot. This was similar to the camera scenario. At this point, I knew I had to do something about her narcissist paranoia and mood swings or, as was more often the case, mood bursts! Whenever I mentioned a psychiatrist or counselor, she would only respond that I was the one needing one, not her.

Then some things happened that gave me the incentive to do something drastic—force her to see a psychiatrist. Her oldest son, who was also a preacher at our church, got caught having sexual intercourse with our video/TV director's daughter. To my surprise, this incident didn't seem to bother my wife too much. She appeared to think it was not so terrible. This surprised me greatly. When her son was forced to repent in front of the church leadership at a business meeting in order to continue to be a minister, she thought it too harsh. His three-year probation, she thought, was wrong also. I told her it was proper. She didn't like that.

In addition, her other son was a bartender and was living with a girl who also was a bartender. She didn't think this was bad either. In fact, she really hit it off with his girlfriend. It was clear to see that she had a drastic double standard. She and her sons could do what they wanted, but my son and I had to be on constant alert lest a woman be within sight or appear on the TV. It was also a sin for me to drink, but not for her son. (At this point, I was not drinking. In fact, I hadn't had a drink for over thirty years.)

Her sons could commit adultery and live with bartenders, but my son couldn't have the girls' softball team over for pizza along with his basketball team. When the girls came to the house, she had a fit, thinking it was improper for girls to be with boys. He was a sophomore in high school! She could also wear a bikini in public, but it wasn't okay for other women to do the same, as my eyes would be drawn to them. Her tight pants, short skirts, and low tops were only okay on her body, not the bodies of other women. Her sons could bring over off-color videos, and she would laugh along with them. However, if *The Beverly Hillbillies* or another show with a woman in it came on TV, I was not allowed to watch it as it was unchristian of me to do so and my son should not see such things. That was it. I did something drastic.

The following Sunday evening, our assistant pastor preached a sermon. In it, he said, "If what you have been doing is not working, try something else!" I had been trying to influence my wife to get help. She would not. Her conduct was not only testing my sanity, but it was also affecting my son. Sure, he was now sixteen years old, but he still needed much guidance during these trying teenage years. At this point, he couldn't even have a girlfriend without my wife having a fit. (I found out later he did but was afraid to tell us.)

One evening later that week while we were lying in bed, I brought up the topic. She insisted she did not need help. I said, "If you don't see a psychiatrist to get your medication in line and help you, I will divorce you."

Immediately, she got up and began putting on her clothes. I knew she would take off in the car, and this time I was confident she would get into a terrible accident. She was shaking and looked like she was going to have a nervous breakdown. I held on to her to try to comfort her, but she would not have it. Finally, I forcefully held on to her for fear she may hurt herself. I made her promise she would not take off if I let her go. She promised. But as soon as I let go, she stormed into my son's bedroom and told him I was divorcing her. At this, my son began crying and carrying on. At this point, he still didn't understand her sickness. He knew she had a problem, because he and his friends called her psycho, but to him she was still his stepmom. I did force him to accept her, and he did—but I found out later this was not a good thing to do. A child should not call his stepmom Mom in a situation like ours. But I had no idea of that at the time.

Now I had two situations on my hands. I tried calming everyone down the best I could, but it was not working. My wife called her oldest son to come over. I called the pastor, hoping he could at least talk some sense into them. He did, and things finally settled down. It was soon thereafter that my son realized the severity of her problem and why I had to force her to see a psychiatrist. Please understand, I did not want a divorce. I loved my wife dearly, but I could not take her paranoia anymore and had to take extreme actions. To this day, I wish I had not mentioned divorce to her, but I also do not know what else I could have done to force her to seek help. There must have been something else I could have done, but I do not know what. This act on my part, I believe, took a piece out of my wife's heart that could never properly be replaced. I had mentioned the forbidden word—*divorce.*

A few months passed, and she still would not get help. So, I filed for divorce. In the midst of this situation, my plant closed due to the economic failure in 2008/9. I had worked there for thirty years. Six years before the closing they stopped contributing to my pension fund. It is ironic, starting at age fifty is when the company contributed the heaviest to the fund. I was only forty-nine when they stopped, so my pension was small. Ten years before this closure, I had quit and accepted a great opportunity at a local hospital as director. What pension I did have at the time I rolled over into a 401k. The golden opportunity, however, was short lived, and within a year, I was back at my old plant again. The opportunity was lucrative, and the company gave me a 20 percent raise to come back, so the move wasn't all that bad. However, it also meant that most of my pension was in a 401k, what little that was. In addition, a few years before the pension stopped, the company had filed bankruptcy, and the stock I had accumulated for more than twenty years became useless. I had lost much of my pension and all of my stock. Nonetheless, I still had close to a quarter of a million in my 401k, so I wasn't worried. It's just that I wouldn't be able to retire till age sixty-five or later. Many of my retirement dreams were shattered, but not lost. Not yet, anyway.

I mentioned earlier that I had to refinance my house to get that darn built-in swimming pool. I also mentioned that we went on a lot of extravagant vacations, and I wasn't saving for my son's college, but figured I could dip into my 401k if I had to. But now I had lost my job, of which I hadn't dreamt could happen. Living in southeastern Michigan during this downturn meant I could not find another job, but I didn't understand that at the time. I was confident I would find another one fairly easily. I kidded around saying I hoped I could have a few months of vacation before landing a job, so I could enjoy life as best I could, considering my circumstances. However, there were no jobs to get, as I would realize during the next couple of years.

My wife did finally agree to see a psychologist, but not a psychiatrist. Because I now understood the difference, that was fine with me. However, she would not go alone but said I had to come with her. That was also fine with me. She found one who was recommended by the Dr.

Dobson website. We went. The psychologist soon realized my wife had a drastic problem. When she questioned my wife concerning these issues, my wife walked out. But before I left the office, the counselor gave me a book to read. It was, *I Hate You—Don't Leave Me* by Jerold J. Kreisman and Hal Straus.[41] It was a small book on the mental disorder called borderline personality disorder. When I returned the book, I told the psychologist the authors were talking about my wife. She told me clearly that if that was the case, I had little hope for my wife's healing, as most people with this disorder, including my wife, would not accept they had a problem and would not get help. Also, marriages with such person's seldom survive. But I was set to prove that theory wrong (actually, it was a fact, not a theory).

My wife said she wanted to see a different psychologist, as the present one was only taking my side. She wanted one who dealt with marriage counseling issues, because it was I who needed the counseling, not her. So, she found another psychologist at a local church who was also approved by the Dr. Dobson website. Again, my wife claimed this new psychologist was taking my side, but she agreed to continue with her anyway. I was now close to cancelling the divorce, as it looked like my wife may be sticking with this psychologist, even though she didn't like her. But before I had a chance to do so, my wife left me. This would be our first separation, and it would last one and a half years.

# The Separation

We were in bed one morning while my son was in the bedroom across the hall, and her youngest son was in the bedroom right next to ours. Her son, now 30, had been fired from his job again and needed a place to stay—for the fourth time. That morning my wife and I got into an argument. She stormed out of the bedroom and into the living room. I took off for the cigar shop. I hadn't smoked in thirty-five years, but she was driving me up a wall, so I began smoking imported handmade cigars after I threatened divorce but before she agreed to see a psychologist. After finishing my cigar, my sister called and said my wife had just talked to my dad and told him I beat her and she was afraid of me. He told her to get a grip and that I did no such thing. Because he wouldn't come over (which would have been very odd except that she was claiming I abused her; of course, he knew she was lying), she drove to the emergency room and told them I beat her. When I arrived, the ER clerk and the guard said I could not go into her room. She was with her two sons (one of which had been in the bedroom next to ours during our argument), and neither she nor they wanted me in. After realizing the guard really was not going to let me see my wife, I went home very angry.

About an hour later, she and her two sons arrived at the house. Her sons called me every name in the book of cusswords and helped her pack. My son and I, both of us very perturbed, began to help her pack also. She left with her two boys. She wouldn't reply my calls or emails for a couple of months. I was devastated. Although I hadn't had any alcohol in thirty-five years, I now began to drink. Then finally, after multiple texts, voice mails, and e-mails from me, she agreed to a date.

# Dating Again

My wife seldom saw my son (who was about 17 years old) during our separation. When she did call or text him, he never responded. The only time she saw him was on special occasions, and then it was at a restaurant, as she did not want me around. Although he didn't want to go, I would tell him she'd have a present and his two stepbrothers would be there, which then prompted him to go. I wanted him to try and get closer to her. I was trying to get her back and, therefore I wanted him to get used to her again.

Finally, we started to date. After a few of these, it looked as though she would come back home. However, when I mentioned this to my son, he went berserk. By this time, he had realized how normal life was again with her gone. He would have no part of her coming home. In addition, she not only left me, but she had left him.

I told my wife that before she moved back home, she and I need to come up with a plan to ease her back with my son. However, as was her way of doing things, the next day she just showed up at the house while my son and I were in the living room. With a big smile on her face, she walked in carrying a bag of donuts in one hand and a bag of burgers in the other. She had gotten me and my son lunch and dessert and was ready to move back in.

Two things shrilled though my mind and body as she walked in. First, I was so glad to see her and thought things may get back to normal (or, as normal as things can be with her). Second, and immediately thereafter, even before my son saw her, I thought, *What the heck are you doing? I just told you yesterday we needed to ease you back with my son!* As soon as she entered the living room, my son got up without a word and went into his bedroom. After an hour or so, she left, happy as a jaybird.

As soon as she left, my son came out of the bedroom, ranting and raging even worse than the day before, veins popping out of his forehead and neck. He said, "Dad, if she moves back in, I'm moving in with Grandpa and Grandma!"

I was between a tough rock and a hard place. I wanted my doll to come back home, but how could I force my only son, who had gone through hell with her for years, to accept back a loony who had left him nothing but joy after she left? I could not do that and be a good father and responsible human being. So, I called her that afternoon to tell her to wait a couple of weeks before moving in. She did not answer, so I left a voice mail. In it, I told her to spend the next couple of weeks trying to make amends with my son and then move in. However, that is not what she heard. What she heard was, "I do not want you to move back in, after all." I know this, because she immediately called our psychologist, crying her eyeballs out, and telling her I didn't want her anymore. The psychologist asked to hear the voice mail. After hearing it, she told my wife that I didn't say that at all. I only wanted her to get used to my son for a couple of weeks before moving in because he was very distressed about it. To this, my wife hung up and never visited that psychologist again. Also, she did not try to get close to my son. Rather, she decided not to move back in. She stopped returning my messages. I was devastated a second time.

As mentioned earlier, I began smoking cigars when she would not see a psychologist and began to drink after she left me. And once started, I began to drink heavily. Vodka, rum, and brandy were my favorites. I mostly drank at home, but once in a while, I'd go to the bar down the road, but never late at night. I did not want to meet another girl. I was just miserable. I drank beer also. I had lost my wife, my son was distressed, my job had vanished, and now my money had run out. My coveted summer vacation had turned into a lingering nightmare from hell.

# Divorce, No Divorce, Divorce, No Divorce

Since my plan of filing for divorce to force her to get professional help only helped temporarily, I cancelled the divorce. My attorney warned me, saying the time to divorce was now; while I was laid off, alimony would be minimal. I was surprised that alimony was still paid by the husband. I thought with the women's movement, the woman would be forced to get a job after a divorce, but that is not the case. The amount paid by the husband (or, in rare cases, the wife) is based on both salaries combined. (Because my wife made peanuts, hers would account for little.) If I divorced while not working, my payments would be small.

The lawyer also stated it was a good thing I didn't live in Ohio, because they had more strenuous laws there. But because I didn't want a divorce in the first place, these things didn't matter. Besides, my wife had made it clear to me that if we did divorce, she didn't want any assets or alimony. Either way, my divorce tactics weren't working. Even though she did go to a psychologist, she had now stopped. (In addition, the appointments appeared to make her worse. The psychologists would ask her to think back on her childhood. This would distress her so bad that she said she felt like she was losing her mind.) And now, she had left me. What good were the divorce papers if they were no longer getting me what I needed?

Certainly, you as the reader must be befuddled by this logic. But remember, I stated above that I only threatened divorce to force my wife to seek help. It was my last resort, or at least, I didn't know of any other resorts. So, I cancelled the divorce and continued to try and talk my wife into coming back home. And now, it would be very difficult, because she needed to make things right with my son first.

Months passed, but there was still no movement from her. So, I did what I do best when a marriage is on the rocks. I filed for divorce again. But this time it was not to force her to seek help, but rather to force her to come back home. It worked. We began dating again. So, I cancelled the second divorce proceedings. If you are counting, this was the second set of divorce papers I began because I didn't want a divorce! Are you following?

# Now, My Head Is Spinning

Let me recap. Within the span of about eight months, I told my wife I would file for divorce if she didn't seek help. She would not, so I began smoking cigars and actually filed for divorce. She decided to see a counselor, but before I had a chance to cancel the divorce, she left, stating I physically abused her. (Of course, I didn't touch her, but the men in her past did. She only imagined abuse after we had an argument.) A month or two later, she showed up at the house unexpectedly, and when my son just about blew a gasket, I asked her to patch things with him before coming back. She heard something different than what I really said and quit the psychologist. I canceled the divorce, realizing it was doing no good. I began to drink. When she consistently refused to come back, I refiled for divorce. When she started dating me again, I cancelled the second divorce. Okay, you should be up to speed now.

During all of this turmoil, I continued to drink heavily. I could not find another job, because there were none to be found. I had a mortgage and high credit card bills. (Remember the vacations?) In my distress, I pulled almost all of my money from the 401k to pay off the mortgage and high bills. This allowed me to breathe a little easier, and I now began sleeping most of the night. I was still distressed because my wife was still gone, but at least I didn't have any bills. As for my retirement, that was the least of my worries at that time. I just wanted my wife back and didn't want to lose my house.

# The Return

One day, while riding my motorcycle around town, I decided to look at sports cars. I did not plan to buy one. I couldn't afford it. I was doing what I had done after my wife died a number of years earlier. Back then, just for something to do, my son and I would go to the Harley shops just to look around. (Of course, I ended up buying one.) This time, I went to car lots and looked at sports cars. Then I saw a great deal—a Porsche convertible for only two-thirds its value. This was just like my Harley deal a number of years earlier. Some people would claim God was with me, and He found this deal for me. But it wasn't that; I just fell into a good deal. Granted, if my family was starving and I fell upon a bunch of food, I would claim inspiration but this was a pleasure vehicle. I bought it. I used the remaining balance in my 401k. Yes, it was extremely stupid, even dumber than paying off my house and bills with it, but I was in such misery, I didn't think that far ahead. When I drove it, I did get some temporary relief from my misery. It was a similar feeling to riding my Harley after my wife died, but not as dramatic.

Then it happened. I received a call for a job opportunity. It was to serve as Chair of the Information Technology School at a technical college. But it was in Akron, Ohio, almost three hours away. I took the job. During the week, I stayed in a cheap apartment and came home on the weekends. My son was a high school senior, so he was old enough to stay home alone. After graduating, he received a partial scholarship to play baseball at a private college only twenty-five minutes from the house. Since he was so excited about it and I was not thinking clearly, I told him he could go. I bought him a car so he could commute. I had always told him that if he lived at home during his college years, I'd buy him a car, figuring it would be cheaper than a dorm. Eventually, I figured, I'd find a job in Michigan again and move back home full time.

As stated above, my wife and I began seeing each other again. I told her to move to Akron with me, but she would have no part of an apartment while my son lived in a nice house in Michigan. She began looking at houses in the area. One day, she showed up at my school and said she had a surprise for me. She had found her dream home. I agreed, because it was the only way I could get her to come back to me. However, we couldn't get a mortgage until we sold our house in Michigan. My son begged me not to sell, but I wanted my wife back. Besides, in a few years, he'd be moving out anyway. My wife continued to search and find a mortgage company that would accept us. Finally, she did, and we bought a home. It was a different dream house than she picked out the first time, however. Her dreams changed often.

Things went pretty good the first year. My wife's episodes appeared to be much milder than they were in the past. But then stressful times came, and I could see the potential for an explosion.

# Beginning of the End

Her first stress crack began when the water line on the refrigerator ice maker broke and partially flooded the basement. The water ran directly down the stairwell wall and onto the basement floor. It saturated the drywall and the carpet. We had just painted and carpeted the whole interior of our house, basement, and garage. My wife had just finished decorating and hanging curtains and blinds. Finally, we could take a well-deserved break and enjoy our new home. But because I was the one who had hooked up the water line, which then leaked into the basement, she thought I was trying to destroy it. She was confident I did it intentionally. She couldn't have anything nice before, so why should she now? It broke her heart to think I didn't want her to have anything nice. This made me mad, so I closed the valve and never did hook it back up. I dried up the basement and redid the sections that were destroyed by water. When done, the basement was as good as new.

The next incident concerned gas fumes in the house. Our new house only had a hook up for a gas stove, but my wife wanted an electric one. Because it would have been very expensive to run an electrical line, I talked her into using gas. One day she came home from work and smelled gas.

She called the fire department, and they found the stove burner was partly turned on. She said I was trying to gas her and wouldn't speak to me for days.

The following additional incidents took their toll on her. She wanted to take care of the bills. I gladly approved. However, it caused her much stress. I could see it and knew I should take them over, but she was doing such a good job that I hated to. She was also proud of the fact she was doing a good job, and I told her so.

Because my son's dorm and living expenses were becoming more than we could afford, I told him I would have to renege on the vacant lot I gave him and sell it to pay for them.[42] He told me he was okay with it. Actually, it was to our advantage because the sale of the lot would not only pay for his living expenses but also a good part of his college. Since my son's college was such a strain on my wife, I thought this would relieve her a bit, but it did not.

Another situation occurred that helped put her over the edge. Her preacher son had become engaged to a woman my wife did not like. Because of this, she and her son were not getting along. This wore her out. She would continuously fast and pray over this. She did this so much that it was taking a toll on our marriage. I told her to let up a bit as I could not live like a hermit. She locked herself up in a room for days at a time. When he finally did break up with the girl, his now ex-fiancé did everything she could to get him into trouble. At one point, she had a restraining order put on him and tricked him into seeing her at the mall. She called the police, and he spent the night in jail. To say the least, their breakup was even more stressful on my wife than when they were together, so she continued her constant fasting and prayer. Fasting and praying is good, but not when it is detrimental to a marriage, and that is what was happening. Then the line almost broke.

My wife's son's ex-fiancé called me at work. She talked a mile a minute as she told me how my wife's son had treated her badly. It was all nonsense so I was ready to hang up, but then she said something that caught my attention. It sounded like she said, "Your wife told me to get an abortion and said it wasn't so bad because she had had one." I asked her to repeat it, but the cell phone began to break up and then disconnected. I waited a minute for her to call back, but she did not. So, I called her. I asked her to repeat what she had said. I heard her correctly. After a minute, I hung up.

I didn't tell my wife what I'd been told right away, because she was going through another of her episodes. When she was almost over it, probably a day or so later, I told her of my conversation. She acted uncomfortable when I told her, but then she began to laugh and said, "She's nuts, isn't she?" It was forgotten until I got home from work that evening. I worked late that night, so my wife was in bed when I got home.

When I went into the bedroom, immediately, my wife said very disgustingly, "Why did you call her?" She had gone online and looked at the cell phone calls. It showed I called her son's ex-fiancé back. My wife was furious. I tried to explain the fact that I lost connection at a critical moment and needed to find out if she was pregnant. My wife would have none of it. As far as she was concerned, I just wanted to talk to her and get dirt on my wife. She slept in the spare bedroom for the next week or so.

I wrote it off as another episode but began to wonder what the real reason for her anger was. Did she have an abortion? I did not believe she did, but as I write today, I now wonder. The way she laughed it off that morning but then became so angry the following evening—why? What did she do that time she took off for twenty-four hours claiming to only spend the night in the hotel room?

Her episodes were becoming more frequent and more intense. They were also becoming very similar to the ones she had before leaving me the first time. I began to wonder if I'd find her gone when I got home from work one day. In my memoirs, I noted the possibility of that fact. (These things were going on during the writing of part one of this book.) Then she accused me of rummaging through her desk drawers. Her paranoia was becoming out of control again. She said she was going to put cameras in the house like I had at the old house. (If you remember, this is what she claimed I did before she left me the first time.)

# The Neighbor Lady

I came home from work early one day to get the grass cut. The neighbor lady was in her side yard planting shrubs. My wife, when she came home from work, saw me cutting the lawn on the side of our house where the neighbor was planting the shrubs. She came up to me and gave me the first degree, asking a hundred questions as to why I was cutting the grass on that side of the house. I told her to get inside and said I'd talk to her later. After the grass was done, I went into the house and asked my wife what her problem was. She said I was looking up the skirt of the neighbor lady. I told her they were shorts, and in addition, why would I look at the neighbor when my wife was much prettier? She didn't buy it and was convinced she had a skirt on and not shorts. Believe it or not, a couple of weeks later, I asked the lady and she told me they were skorts, which look like a skirt from front but are really shorts. I know she thought I was loony, so I talked to her husband the next day and tried to explain. They are nice people, but I have to believe they think they have a real nut job as a neighbor.

The six weeks before my wife left (this second and final time) were very rough. My wife's stress with bills, her son's wedding breakup, and dealing with the nut job of an ex-fiancé was very hard on her. Her other son thought he had heart problems but found out it was only stress during all of this. She was convinced I was spying on her by going into her desk drawers and thought I was looking up the neighbor lady's skirt. These and other things stretched her paranoia to the limit. I had to do something. But what?

# Then Snap

It was the day before Mother's Day. My wife always gets stressed on Mother's Day. (Many years ago on this day, I noted a disgusted look on her face. I asked her what was wrong. She said, "F—— you!" and went into the bedroom.) Mother's Days were always hard on her when her boys were not around. They became especially bad after her mother died. This Mother's Day would be our last together.

I already talked about the flowers her son sent the day before and my trip to celebrate my parent's sixtieth wedding anniversary earlier in this book. Her terrible sobbing that Mother's Day tore my heart out of my chest. But I could only tell her I didn't do anything and she was only imagining her past.

# The End

The next morning, she left for her new job. This was to be her first day. She worked Mother's Day on her old one. I had tried to talk her out of it, but she worked anyway. I did not try to figure that out. She didn't kiss me when she left. She would always kiss me, no matter how mad she was at me.

I had a late class that day, so I didn't get home from work till after ten o'clock that night. When I opened the garage door, her car was gone. I knew she had left. I called and texted her that afternoon, but she would not reply. I texted her again, asking where she was. She said she went to her son's house, which was three hours away in Michigan, because she missed him. I was so perturbed at her for traveling three hours away without a word and not answering me in the afternoon that I did not reply.

I found out months later that she had taken more than fifty thousand dollars from my accounts just minutes after she texted me, all the while claiming she was just visiting her son because she missed him. The next evening she texted me again, stating she didn't get to visit much the day before, so she was staying another day. I didn't answer her text, figuring I'd give her some of her own medicine. I haven't seen her since.

During the course of the next few weeks, she would not answer my calls or texts. Finally, I asked her how to cook corned beef. She texted with the instructions and then said she didn't know if she was coming home. It was two days later when I got home from work that I found the house was empty. She even took the curtain rods and mounts. I went to the bank to figure out what accounts we had, because I now had to take care of bills. This was when I found she had taken ten thousand dollars from savings and fifty thousand dollars from another account. My attorney is trying to get the money back, but I don't have much hope for it. I had to file a restraining order and a divorce.

# Divorce

I now come to the end of my story. I am in the middle or, rather, close to the end of my divorce with the doll I married almost twelve years ago. I thought she was Help, but my Help has turned into a nightmare. What few assets I have left, she is going after with tooth and nail. It almost appears that today's court systems challenge women to divorce their husbands if they don't like him anymore or if he sits at the kitchen table wrong. If he isn't the desire of her life in every aspect, she can leave him and take everything he has. But that is neither here nor there as far as you, the reader, are concerned. You don't know me, and many, if not most, men deserve it. But my complaint is that not all do. Therefore, the courts should still determine fault. Nonetheless, I now have a mortgage, which I did not have before, bills from replacing my furniture and such, the equity line of credit she took, and now alimony. I don't know what I am going to do.

My finances are now devastated. I have no savings. I have very little in a retirement fund and no pension. My wife left me, and I am alone in Akron. But, here's the punch line. She is claiming I physically abused her on that dreadful Mother's Day. The fact is, she was reliving her youth during this episode and replaced me with the horrible men of her past. Her sobbing was a reenactment of what she had done time and time again before she met me. Once she did meet me, I was God because someone finally treated her well.

However, when I began to disagree with her because she falsely accused me of things, in her eyes, I became those men of her past. My slightly raised voice became the woman beater she had been used to. My presence when a woman was nearby was transported into her past experience with her brother and her ex-husband. She was seeing a false reality. And because of that, she is now causing my nightmare. She told her attorney that she has spent every penny of the money she took from me and is living in Florida. She says she needs spousal support during the interim of our divorce due to my beating her and causing her to be unable to work.

I received a letter the other day (*approximately 8 months after she left me this final time and 4 months before our divorce*) stating the court will be taking a good chunk of my check for her, starting this week, even though we hadn't had the pretrial yet. I also have to pay back temporary alimony for the past five months. I don't know how I am going to make it. I do hope and pray I don't have to sell my house. The final divorce trial date is set for six weeks from now. I expect she won't have to pay back the money she took and I will give her almost half of my check. I am thinking about getting a boarder so I don't have to sell my house.

# My Life

Well, folks, the divorce is still proceeding. That woman has devastated me. She has not destroyed me, however. Yes, she is a major cause of my financial demise. She did put me on a roller coaster ride that gave me thrills and chills. She did deceive me into thinking she was Help when, in fact, she was Destruction.[43] She did cause me to leave work or class early, time and time again, because she was depressed and/or having problems with my son (which were made up). She did cause me stress when she stopped at garage sales and stores on the way home from work instead of getting home when my son got home from school when he was only nine and ten years old. She did send a text to my coworker stating I physically abused her that dreadful Mother's Day, but she would always love me and will carry my name to the grave.

Yes, bipolar actions as these were daily occurrences in my life with her. In fact, just the other day, she called my pastor and told him how I had treated her terribly but was basically a good guy. She only called so he would know to pray for me! Out of her mouth proceeds grains and thistles, angelic words and demonic words, all in the same sentence. It *will* be in my best interest to be in the poorhouse and all alone. My nightmare life with a borderline, paranoid narcissist is almost over, except for the alimony. My borderline wife has deserted me. I would have rather lived out our lives together. I did promise for better or for worse. But she left me, lied about me, and is now stealing from me. Everyone tells me I am better off, but it doesn't feel that way. This past weekend I did feel more normal than I had in a long time. Now, I may know what my son felt like after she left the first time. Normality. That would be nice. I had forgotten what normal felt like. However, I will not be able to forget our good times.

There were a lot good times, many of which I've not put into these pages. The time she stood at the bathroom window with no clothes on, shaking her breasts while I was in the back yard is etched in my memory. I'd look around to ensure no one was looking and then look back at her as she smiled like an angel. And there was the time we made a porn movie, where she actually got into it so much that she had an orgasm. I loved watching that part. I destroyed the film after about a year, fearing if something happened to us, the kids may find it. Part of me wishes I still had it. Part of me wishes I had more pictures of her in her bikini. I do have lots of pretty pictures of her with her angelic smile. I haven't figured out what I will do with those yet.

My times with her were either spectacular or devastating. I have no memories of any in between or normal states. There were none. There was only eggshell walking, or splashing, bliss or torment. I need to be "normal" again. I think I will. Actually, I have no choice. I hope that's a blessing.

# PART IV

# On the Borderline

Just now, I changed the heading above from "The End" to "Part IV." I was finished with my book. However, this morning, which happens to be the day of my pretrial when my attorney and my wife's attorney will tell the judge what assets we expect of each other, I began to ponder my wife's future. I think I know what my future will be. But hers? I have no idea.

Will she find someone else to make her happy for a short period of time before he realizes he cannot live with her, much like her last two husbands (of which I am number two)? Will she wallow in her sorrow for years, wondering why God did this to her? How long will it take for her friends and family to realize she was the one who caused our demise and not me? Or, will they continue to believe their sweet, innocent sister, mother, or friend? I don't know the answer to these questions, and to be honest, I'm not extremely concerned how they pan out. I do hope she finds happiness, though. I am fully convinced her present dilemma is not her fault.

As I continued to ponder, I went to my basement to look for the borderline personality disorder books I had purchased, read, and studied over the past few years. I had hidden them in a moving box, as I did not want my wife to see them. This morning, however, I figured I may as well put them on my bookshelf, because she will never be here again except to pick up the rest of her clothes and whatever else she can take. Ever since my wife stormed out of the office of the first psychologist we went to and I was given the book, *I Hate You—Don't Leave Me*,[44] I have been convinced she has BPD. I continued to buy books on the disorder and now have a few. I began to leaf through these books, most of which are somewhat scholarly and of which I will speak about in the following pages. I recall how accurate the traits in the books reflected my wife and me. Although she has not been diagnosed, I am a firm believer she has this disorder with a good dose of paranoid and narcissistic disorders, which BPD people sometimes have.

Before delving very deep into these books, however, I looked on the Internet to see if any new material had been written on the topic. Of course, there is a lot. Actually, there is a lot of information on everything on the Internet. Therefore, the following pages will be devoted to my books and internet findings. In my search, I happened upon an intriguing article. It fit my marriage with my wife so perfectly that I just had to add part four to this book. The article was in the Facing the Facts[45] website, which is devoted to people like me who live with a loved one with BPD and is endorsed by the author of the book I was first given by our psychologist. I will title this next section:

# Marriage on the Borderline

In his Facing the Facts article titled, "How a Borderline Personality Disorder Love Relationship Evolves,"[46] which is based on the book, *Romeo's Bleeding* by Roger Melton, M.A., I saw my wife and I over the course of our twelve years together. Below, I will mention sections of his book as I discuss my relationship with my wife, as the book and my marriage were not much different from each other.

Borderlines will alter their appearance to please others. My wife had her nose redone because her dad had called her big nose as a child. She also dyed her hair blonde and highlighted it. She also wore a lot of makeup. Don't get me wrong; she did not look gaudy but quite the contrary. I didn't know her hair was dyed or that she wore much makeup till later. She looked like a Barbie doll. She attended the gym often and had a body that would win any beauty pageant.

My wife went through three stages during our marriage. First it was Vulnerable Seducer, then the Clinger, and then the Hater. Her present stage, the Hater, is shown in her wanting to take me to the cleaners, even though a few years ago she didn't want anything if we were to divorce. I will discuss these three stages below.

When we first met, she was in her Vulnerable Seducer phase. She was so sweet and shy and in need of being rescued. She called me her knight in shining armor, and I called her my damsel in distress. In fact, she wrote me a poem. It starts out,

> Knight,
> I love you … because you're my love, my precious hero.

It continues on and ends with,

> I was a damsel in distress, but God heard my prayers and gave me the best.
>
> Your Doll.

Around those poetic lines she tells how she dreamt of someone like me who might sweep her off her feet and show her true happiness. I was handsome with bright armor and would rescue her if she should fall. She also kids around a bit, as we often did, and says how she couldn't wait to make whoopee when I got home from work. To this very day, I still carry that poem in my wallet. I can't throw it away. I used to get shrills when I read it. Now I get stomach cramps. It still brings tears to my eyes, however.

She used to tell me that I was the only one who really understood her. Her friends, many of which betrayed her, and even family members didn't hold a candle next to me, her hero. I was special and not like the other guys she had dated before and very unlike her ex-husband and especially her brother and dad. She used to say she put me before God. I was her god. Our relationship was so intense when we talked, ate, or especially when we made love. She used to tell me my speeches and articles were awesome. She was just too good to be true.

Next came the Clinger Phase. According to Melton, although she still was very interested in me, that interest changed into how much interest she thought I had in her. We were only married a few days when she began to transition into this phase. Suddenly, she was very adamant that I only pay attention to her and no other. If a pretty woman walked by, I wasn't paying enough attention to her. After our honeymoon, she thought I paid too much attention to my son and not enough to her. Before our marriage, I spent time with him when she was away so when she was with me I could devote most time to her. However, once we married and she was always at the house, she saw me paying attention to my son, hence her concern. She wanted me only to herself and no one else. Our weekend trip to an amusement park without my son is a case in point.

Whenever I paid undivided attention to her alone, she was happy. She treated me so wonderfully and tenderly when I only had eyes on her. But if she saw my eyes wonder somewhere else, watch out! Because I wanted to rescue her from her demise of poverty and despair, it was my one-way emotional rescue that I mistook for real love. I needed to help her. She only wanted me to adore her. I loved her. I still do, and I can't help it, no matter how much I try to listen to my reason and the reason of others.

During this phase, physical complaints were common. Her legs hurt, and she had to have a built-in pool to relieve them. Her coworkers did not do their part, and she had to work extra hard to make up for their laziness. One time the psychologist asked me if she complained a lot. I thought for a minute, and as if I had been enlightened, I said, "Yes, all the time!" I just knew I could help her, though, but I could not. My effort to understand and help her was, as Melton says in his article, "an excruciatingly pointless exercise in emotional rescue." I was "pouring myself into a galactic sized Psychological Black Hole of bottomless emotional hunger!"[47] I would save her from the dragon only to have her stab me in the back for saving her. She would jump back off the horse so the dragon could chase her again so I would save her from the dragon and ... over and over again. Melton says, eventually, I will fall into that black hole of despair. Thanks, I wish I had realized that before I fell.

Sex will be incredible during this period, according to the article. No kidding? I have empirical evidence of that, and I still don't know if it was worth it. It should be a no-brainer, but sometimes certain things are worth the cost. I've still to determine that. She swept me away with her erotic passion, but I've already told you about that. According to Melton, when she said, "I love you," what she really meant was, "I need you to love me."

Then the final phase, The Hater, reared its ugly head. She became furious about things that appeared obvious to her but had no basis in reality to anyone else. Case in point: when she stayed at the hotel swimming pool all day when I complimented her by saying she reminded me of her mom. To her, I was saying she was old and ugly.

No matter what I did, it was wrong. I never knew what to do next. When I came home late from work, I never knew whether to kiss her while she lay in bed or to quietly get in bed without making a sound. It never failed over the past couple of years, if I kissed her, I woke her up and she couldn't go back to sleep all night, and hence was mad at me the whole next day. But if I quietly got into bed, she believed I didn't love her because I didn't kiss her when I got home!

I tried to do what I could to get her back to the clinger stage and often did. But it was just a matter of time before she hated me again. Hate stages especially occurred during holidays. The last one was this past Mother's Day (*when my wife left me of which I have spoken often*). Melton says, "Borderline Personality Disorder is a serious mental illness."[48] No kidding? It destroyed my life.

# Unfulfilled Intensity

In the article, "Sex on the Edge" by Gina Piccalo,[49] a man she interviewed said of his BPD girlfriend that she fills the intensity missing in his life. It is a fact; my present wife filled a void that was there because my first wife did not much enjoy sex due to her hormonal disorder. Piccalo further describes my wife when she describes the borderline woman as dead sexy with ferocious impulses. This woman is irresistible. Irresistible is an understatement when it came to my wife. She and I attracted like a magnet on steel, the pope on Catholicism, or more appropriately, fruit flies on a rotten banana! You get the picture.

"The fourth edition of the Diagnostic and Statistical Manual of Mental Disorders … says, 'Frantic attempts to avoid real or imagined abandonment, chronic feelings of emptiness, difficulty controlling anger and transient, stress-related paranoia are other indications of BPD.'"[50] The article further states that many borderlines suffered child sex abuse and grow up in desperate need for control. Lots of time is spent on outward appearance. My wife certainly falls into this category.

Peter Freed, assistant professor of psychiatry at Columbia University, says that being beautiful causes others to treat you like an object, and this can make you long for confirmation.[51] I had to confirm her beauty and say I loved her multiple times per day, or she would fall into a deep state of depression that was very hard to get her out of. Freed goes on to say that a BPD woman may encourage a man's hero complex. Because of the fact that her husband or boyfriend then gains a false sense of importance, it is often the case that narcissistic men are attracted to borderline women.

I don't know if I have narcissistic tendencies or not—I probably do—but it sure did feel good when she called me her knight in shining armor. In fact, all of her e-mails, texts, letters, and birthday cards started with *Knight* and ended with *Doll*. All of mine started with *Doll* or *Babydoll* and ended with *Knight*. The hero complex complemented her beauty and sexual intensity. She was a Barbie doll, but I was much more than Ken. However, her concern for her hero became far too demanding. Her constant questions—Where were you? Why are you twenty minutes late coming home from work?—were exhausting. One time, while on a business trip, she accused me and my coworkers of going to the topless bars. She had no reason to think such a thing. But, if she had seen a program on businessmen going to such places on TV, that would trigger such an episode. These false accusations caused much undue friction between us.

Sometimes borderlines cut themselves to feel just a bit of pain to help relieve the misery they are experiencing. I did often notice her back would be scratched enough that blood had been drawn. I would rub my hand on her back, and her whole back would be covered with these scratches. When asked what caused them, she would always say that she didn't know. The article closes with the fact that one of the guys interviewed stated he was a devil periodically. This is a fact when having a relationship with a woman with BPD. You become an angel or a devil, sometimes multiple times per day.

# Eggshells

One of the books on my shelf that I had read over the past couple of years is titled, *Stop Walking on Eggshells: Taking Your Life Back When Someone You Care about Has Borderline Personality Disorder.*[52] Eggshells is a good term to use. My house had them all over the floor. When I walked, I had to make sure I didn't step on one, because if I did, I had no idea what kind of explosion would happen next. Speaking of a non BPD person, the author of *Eggshells* aligns life with a borderline as an episode of *The Twilight Zone*. He explains that things can be moving along as normal as can be, then all of a sudden—*wham!*—life takes a quantum leap. Normal life suddenly succumbs into a black hole.

The book continues in stating that the nonborderline performs valiant and heroic acts of kindness, no matter what the price to himself. These nonborderlines swallow their anger and accept behavior that others would not tolerate. The same transgressions are forgiven over and over again. However, although these motives are commendable, they often reinforce the borderline's behavior. Another nonborderline described it as feeling like a failure. He just knew he could help his wife, if only he could convince her to get help. Finally, the therapist told *him* that because he was not God he needed to quit beating himself up.

I had thought I could fix my wife over the course of a few years. She had such a miserable past, and I felt so sorry for her; I knew I could put up with anything she threw at me because she would see the light eventually. However, I am not God. It took me a long time to find that out. I had never totally failed before, and I could not believe I would fail this time either. However, I cannot fix what is not fixable. Only God can do that.

In part three of this book, I described how women were a major problem between us. The non-BP Internet support group posted a comment about a husband who told his wife he loved her, that she was beautiful, and that he would never leave her. But, over and over again, she would think she saw him flirting with women in public. If a sales lady talked to him, she'd accuse him of wanting her. But he finally concluded that even the Grand Canyon could never be filled with a water pistol. In the same way, he would never please her.

I recall an incident around five years ago at the Harley Davidson shop. The lady in charge of clothing asked me if I needed help. I told her no and walked away. Quickly, my wife came up to me very upset and told me she was going to beat that lady up for flirting with me. She continued to go on and on about how a stupid lady at the Harley shop was not going to take her husband away from her. She continued her ranting and raging till I finally told her to keep quiet and that the lady was not flirting with me. This was the only time I remember when she did not appear to be mad at me but rather at the woman.

I felt so sorry for my wife. I knew she couldn't help what she was thinking, and her mood swings were heavily due to her terrible past. I loved that woman so much. When she wasn't having a bad day (or, rather, a bad minute), she was so kind, sweet, and adorable. That is what kept me going through the horrendous number of swings to the dark side.

Mason and Kreger go on to say that BPD women often experience depression and a painful yearning for intimacy. I've already described my wife's father. She was often depressed, which is why she'd take Wellbutrin periodically. She often talked of how she wished her dad had taken her up on his lap and stroked her hair like he used to do with her sister. I would often try to fill the void by holding her and stroking her hair for long periods of time. Sometimes, after she had an episode and ran to the spare bedroom to try and get away from it all, I would come in and lie beside her. I'd stroke her hair. Sometimes this would last for an hour or two. It was extremely exhausting, but she enjoyed it and eventually came around again.

But it was my threat of divorce if she did not get help that set her off into a frenzy that she never recovered from. Mason and Kreger[53] explain that when a BP views the spouse's desertion as total, he or she might develop paranoid ideas of betrayal and conspiracy. The BP spouse may then begin to rewrite history, beginning to believe that the partner had intentionally plotted from the beginning to take advantage of and then leave him or her. This is certainly true of my situation. After my wife left me the first time (which was after I threatened divorce) and we were again beginning to date, we began to see yet a third psychologist. These sessions would be different, however. My wife ensured she got the upper hand right away by telling him right off that I was not to meet or talk to him without her present. This caused me to pay $125 each for two sessions we did not go to because she didn't show up. He wouldn't talk to me but gladly took my mandatory $125 for not cancelling twenty-four hours in advance!

But the real change was in what she said. She had always misperceived reality, but now she was changing history 180 degrees. She told him she could not live with me because I wanted to use sex toys (which we hadn't done in a couple of years) and that I went to the stores to buy them against her will. When I reminded her that she went to the store near Cedar Point and we went to the others together, she told the psychologist I was lying. She told many other altered historical facts. Of course, the psychologist didn't know who to believe. I stopped the sessions after only a few months because my wife kept cancelling sessions after the deadline and did not do what the psychologist told her to before coming to the next session. I was wasting a lot of money for nothing, so we quit going.

Her conspiracy theories were many. She claimed I had cameras in the house and her car and spyware on her computers. But it was her who continuously watched *my* every move. She went into my desk and briefcase and took files and such. I didn't care, but she was trying to find things. All the while, she would accuse me of getting into *her* things.

Her present fight with me during our divorce trial is also lined with lies. Yesterday at our pretrial she said she was disabled when we met so I should therefore pay her half my wages, as she cannot work. The judge was alarmed when I told him she was working two jobs when we met but quit one to be with me during a dizzy spell and the other one because she claimed her legs hurt. I mentioned these earlier in this book. I could go on and on. But the point is, I am now her archenemy who only married her to try and destroy her. She must now protect herself from a demonic villain.

I had no idea that during her slashes at me, she would continue to do so and even more severely as time went on. Because of my misunderstanding of this, I did not watch out to protect myself. I now wonder if my wife was intent upon buying a house in Ohio because Ohio forces more alimony from the husband than Michigan. (This is what both of my attorneys in Michigan told me.) When she wanted her name on the Porsche, it was not to level out our vehicles in case I died but rather so she could claim it was hers in the event of a divorce, which is what she is doing. But now I may sound paranoid, so I'll end that.

Psychologists do say that nonborderlines begin to take on borderline behavior after living with one for a period of time. I hope I have gotten out in time. Either way, in her eyes, I am not a person who had good qualities in the past. She doesn't remember the good times we used to have. She now only sees an evil monster who deserves to be punished and is ready to establish a distortion campaign.[54] She therefore sees nothing wrong in lying to try to extract every bit of money from me that she can.

# It's a Mystery

I think I'll stop Googling BPD. Instead, I'll continue comparing my marriage with BPD in the books I have. But first, one more Google. The Jezebel site,[55] which I had never heard of till today, makes tongue-in-cheek fun of the fact that there actually may be women out there like my wife. Anna North insinuates that it is a double standard of men who claim this is a problem that women face. She believes that such wives as mine probably don't exist, and even if they do, they coupled up with an equally insane man. Therefore, the phrase "it takes two to tango" is emphasized. She comments that BPD is assigned far more often to woman than to men, and it is therefore stigmatizing to women and stereotypical. Finally, she laments that such articles, books, and movies that emphasize these traits don't help women and assigns it to old-fashioned beliefs such as some of Sigmund Freud's odd conclusions on sexual matters. She says that books on the subject should be written so BPD women can be helped and to help themselves.

I must ask, however, should all books be written so women with borderline personality disorder can know what to do to help themselves? It is a known fact that many of these women, including my wife, do not believe they have a problem in the first place and therefore would not benefit from these books because they won't read them. And what about the psychologists? Certainly, they need these books (as North states) but again, those with BPD often won't see a psychologist in the first place, or at least won't believe what they are told by a psychologist. My wife proves these points.

What does need to be written, however, are books, articles, and movie scripts about people who have BPD and how a loved one is to deal with it. This is precisely what the Jezebel writer is trying to counter. I am certainly no expert, but I do have twelve years of empirical knowledge on the subject. If it weren't for scholarly writings contrary to what Anna North believes, I would probably be half on my way to being a borderline myself. So, to hell with the Anna Norths of the world! People with a BPD loved one also need these books and articles. Journalists with an agenda but little to no knowledge of the subject need to put their pens down and let those who know do the writing.

In Robert O. Friedel's book, *Borderline Personality Disorder Demystified*,[56] he explains what a wife with BPD may be like and how her husband might react. It is so clear to me that he had my wife and me in mind. He tells of a woman who came into his office due to depression and a troubled marriage. She said her husband was going to leave her due to her extreme jealousy and her continual demands for reassurance and attention that led to many arguments. Friedel found out the husband was also very tired of the fact that he could never reason with her due to her responses not making any sense. He also had to come home from work early many times to settle her down. Finally, however, after therapy and medication, their marriage was saved.

If only I could have gotten my wife to admit she may have had a problem, maybe the above couple would be my wife and I today. However, she would only admit that I had a problem, and when she did get antidepressants, they were from our family doctor. When I told her she needed to get them from a psychiatrist, she only said I was telling her she was crazy. The literature and treatment for the BPD patient is there in plenty, contrary to North's nonsensical article. Friedel was able to help not only this woman, but also her husband, and hence, another marriage was saved. No telling who else was impacted if they had children.

Jealousy will extract trust from a marriage, and it wears down the jealous one's partner. Love is a two-way trust. Jealousy chips away at that trust till there is none left. When trust is gone, love is gone. When love is gone, marriages fail. Some fail before that love is gone, as is my case, but fail they do. Where was Friedel when I needed him?

When trying to make my wife understand certain discussion points, it was also very exhausting. I couldn't explain anything to her. We could never have a normal conversation. Her reasoning didn't make sense. And trying to find compromise amid a disagreement? That was out of the question. It was either her way or my way, in which case she would drop into a state of depression. The other option was for me to take her side entirely, even if I knew it was 100 percent wrong. I did that at first, but then I had to be an adult, father, and good citizen. That is when she realized I was no longer prince charming, but rather the dark knight.

Friedel mentioned nightmares. I described some of my wife's dreams earlier in this book. Of course, some of her dreams wouldn't be considered nightmares but simply very strange dreams. Nonetheless, there were many other nightmares that I won't bore you with.

Further in Friedel's book, he goes on to describe the effects of a borderline on the spouse. He says the nonborderline spouse often experiences Elisabeth Kubler-Ross's five stages of grief. They are denial, anger, bargaining, depression, and then acceptance. In addition, the spouse often feels trapped and experiences a loss of self-esteem and takes up unhealthy habits. In fact, it is not uncommon for the spouse to begin to take on borderline-like symptoms him- or herself. Concerning borderlines, they often blame the nonborderline spouses for their problems and say the nonborderline is the one with the issue, not themselves.

This describes my trek with my wife to a tee. Concerning the grieving process, I had a double dose. Below is an email I sent to our second psychologist when we were seeing yet the third and final one (and we were still separated the first time). I was still in contact with the second psychologist for a while and kept her informed of our progress or, more appropriately, regression. I have taken out the names.

> Our first session with [psychologist three] was very good. We set up two more meetings. Mid-November is the earliest he can get us in again. [My wife] is madder than a hornet because of the episode I mentioned the other day. [I don't recall what this episode was.] We met at [the psychologist's] Thursday. She [my wife] looked terrible. This is weird because she reminded me of [my deceased wife] when I first saw her in the casket. Just something about her face and chin that said, "I hate you." I felt that way about [my deceased wife] because until the autopsy I thought I killed her by not getting

> her to the hospital in time. But someone who grieves thinks weird, and that's what I did. Anyway, I can't get over it. As soon as I saw [my present wife] Thursday, her face made me think of [my wife] in the casket. I think it may be a sign. I don't believe in such things, but, in the last 8 or 9 years I've experienced a lot of things I don't believe in!!

Well, I feel like I am grieving again. The psychologist asked [my wife] if she were not a Christian if she would divorce me. She said, very quickly, "Yes." She hates me.

Double dose grief—it doesn't get much worse than that. By the time we went to this third psychologist, I had already taken up the "unhealthy habits" of smoking cigars and drinking too much, but I've already talked about that.

# Getting Inside of Her Head

Finally, I want to talk about another book I read along with the others a few years ago. It was written by Rachel Reiland, a recovering BPD, titled, *Get Me Out of Here.*[57] It is her story of the pain she experienced along with the pain she inflicted on others. I do recall, when I read this book for the first time, how sorry I felt for my wife, realizing the torrential pain she was feeling every minute of every day. I wanted her to get help and be healed.

Reiland wanted to disappear and run away from everything. My wife had told me many times over the years she wished she were dead. How often did she call me at work or at school with a normal situation that she had turned into Mount Everest? I had to run home to save the day. Or the times she took off in the car for hours and would not tell me where she was. Reiland would often call her husband for no apparent reason, or she'd take off and not communicate with him for long periods of time. She didn't realize the torment she put him through. At least once, she went to the hospital without letting her husband know.

How often would my wife go to the emergency room due to stress, depression, and anxiety that caused her blood pressure to drop below a healthy level. She would not call me. Sometimes I wouldn't know it till I got the bill. Reiland had similar instances.

One thing my wife would never agree to was that she may have a problem. One day I didn't hide my books on BPD very well, and she saw them. She went berserk. I don't really recall what all transpired that day, as I am now reminded of the incident from a note I entered into the book I am now discussing. The note marked the page when Reiland found out she had been diagnosed with BPD. She was extremely irate with her therapist, as if her problem was his fault.

My heart tears out again and again whenever I think of the fact that my wife needed constant reassurance that she was good and loving. She would often tell me of compliments she received from coworkers, bosses, or acquaintances. Any time someone gave her a compliment, she held on to it and told me about it. The fact that she continuously needed these tugs at my inner heart. It tears me up. Reiland mentions the fact that borderlines seek love wherever they can find it. They are so needy of other people's approval that they squeeze every ounce of love or affection they can from those individuals. She called it being able to feel safe from harm. Somehow, a borderline needs this reassurance to survive.

Reiland also talks of her sexual desires. They are very much in line with what I had mentioned in part three of this book. I won't elaborate any further on that.

Finally, I've come to the end of my story. I could go on, but I am very tired and even starting to become a bit bored, so certainly the reader must be getting there too. So, it's time to quit. Before doing so, however, I must again mention the book *I Hate You—Don't Leave Me.*[58] It says borderlines sometimes feel they are going insane. They become very frightened by this. Their moods switch back and forth from bliss to extreme depression. The surprise is that there are millions of people like this! I feel extremely sorry for those individuals and their loved ones.

Am I losing my mind? I don't know, but I am losing my sweet borderline personality disorder wife. They say I am better off. I do feel better off. But I don't feel better.

The End (Almost)

# Afterword

It is three days before my final divorce trial date, and I just finished watching *Fatal Attraction*.[59] This was a hit movie in 1987 starring Michael Douglas, Glenn Close, and Anne Archer. I recall my first wife and I watching the VHS in the late eighties and thinking how there was no woman on earth as batty as Glenn Close's character. However, Close actually studied BPD before acting in the film.[60] And, there *is* a woman as batty as Close's character.

I plan to visit the library today or tomorrow and see if they have the movies, *Who's Afraid of Virginia Woolf?*[61] and *Mrs. Parker and the Vicious Circle*.[62] I understand these films also have a borderline star in them. I'll know after I see them.

*Fatal Attraction*'s Glenn Close character portrays my wife with specific differences. These differences especially include my wife's religious character. My wife seldom swore, and then only sparingly, so much so, that I would be shocked when she did. Such an event occurred on a Mother's Day years ago, which I mentioned in my book. She also didn't drink. In fact, she considered alcohol worse than adultery or divorce, again mentioned in my book. One other difference, although I am not positive, was that my wife was not an adulterer, meaning sex outside of marriage while still married. This I can only believe without proof. I gave some instances of this also in my book. All of these differences were due to her religious upbringing and churchgoing practices. However, the other characteristics of Close's character are parallel in likeness.

The first and most obvious thing I noticed when I viewed this movie was how my wife and Glenn Close looked so much alike. I mention it not because it is a borderline similarity but because it is so ironic. If I put my wife's and Close's pictures side by side, a person could swear they were sisters, my wife being the prettier of the two. They both have long blonde and curly hair, but my wife's is thicker and prettier. Both have beautiful bodies, but my wife's is slightly more slender with bigger breasts. But most of all, Close's facial expressions, when she was flirting or disappointed were my wife's all over again. I was flabbergasted!

Other similarities included their wild sex. But yes, you guessed it, ours was more interesting and longer lasting. She was a wild woman (yes, both were). The hooks she put into the life of Douglas's character and family are appropriate. One other difference, however, was Close's character didn't give up when Douglas told her to buzz off. My wife, at least after I told her she had a psychological issue, did give up. Her giving up, however, was leaving me. (I did tell her she had issues due to her childhood. This gradually wore at her and then broke her when I said I'd divorce if she didn't get help.) But, that difference may just have been a fatal difference due to the movie being only two hours compared to my twelve years of marriage. Come to think of it, my wife is now, again, similar to Close's character in that she is trying to sabotage me and my son by taking his college funds and claiming I abused her the day before she left. She is now trying to break me by taking all she can get from my monthly payroll, not to mention what she spent while we were married. So, this is a similarity after all.

The bottom line is that my wife and Close's character each tried to destroy the man she claimed to love. Their flirty, then clinging, and finally destructive behavior are actions only a psychologically unbalanced individual could do. And all in the name of love!

# Conclusion

While glancing out my bedroom window, I see a for-sale sign in the front yard. To the right of me is a king-sized bed with one pillow on it. It's over.

A little over a week ago, on Thursday, I can still hear my ex-wife's attorney yelling at her, stating that she was being unreasonable. Yes, you read that correctly: "her attorney." She was trying to take me to the cleaners and back, and her attorney knew the judge would not buy it. She wanted to keep the sixty thousand dollars she stole from me plus the furniture and everything else she took while I was away at work, plus my 401k, plus my Porsche, and also one thousand dollars per month for four years. She had taken more from my lot equity fund than it was worth and spent all of my savings (this is the vacant lot I mentioned earlier—the bank mistakenly put our home equity loan on this lot). My only asset was my house. She was willing to leave me with that mortgage.

Because I had been aware of this for some time, I began to put feelers out for a new job. Paying my bills and her alimony was more than I could presently afford, so I updated my resume and my LinkedIn profile. A week or so later I received an e-mail from a school in Columbus (one hour and forty-five minutes away) asking if I knew of any instructors who were looking for a job. I initially thought it was the director of our Columbus school and thought I'd respond for my adjunct instructor who was looking for a full-time position.

The e-mail reply noted the school name, and I then knew it was not one of ours. I asked what the salary would be. That reply turned into five interviews and a potential salary increase. By Friday, the day after my divorce, I had received an offer. It was a 27 percent pay increase but would mean I'd either have to commute over an hour and a half or sell my house. I told him I'd have to mull it over the weekend and let him know Monday. Since my ex-wife did not get what she was asking but only eight thousand dollars from my 401k and the money she had already stolen, I really didn't have to take the job immediately.

Saturday morning (yes, the day after the offer letter, which was a day after my divorce) my director called me into her office. She handed me a letter. It was my termination notice! I couldn't believe it. I had grown my school program by 25 percent over the past two years and established our student-run IT club and also formed an IT professional student chapter. My employee reviews all came back excellent. I couldn't believe they were terminating me. Come to find out, Headquarters decided to trim the head count of schools that were under a certain student number. Although my program was as large as or larger than many, the other programs at our campus were small, so our school was considered undersized. Therefore, all chairs were eliminated, no matter who was in that position.

I shook the director's hand, went to my office, signed the offer letter from the Columbus school, and sent it in. I start next week. I will fly to Texas that first week for training. It looks very promising, and the school is growing very nicely.

I picked out an apartment only eight minutes from my new school and put the house and my Porsche up for sale. When my son comes to see me, the apartment will work just fine. If things work out well, I'll look for a house. But this new venture has good potential for advancement, so I may be moving to another state before too long anyway. Apartments may work for me for now.

Next Sunday is Easter. My son turns twenty-one the following Saturday and graduates from college next year. I have a new life. I don't know what the future holds, but I do know Who holds the future. That makes me comfortable.

# Conclusive Note

I must add a note. I am in the air and on my way to Dallas. Last Thursday I sold my Porsche to my attorney. Two days ago, I sold my house for virtually what I was asking for it. It was only up for sale for nine days! My move-out date is the same weekend my new apartment opens up near my new job. The buyer wants to buy most of the stuff in the house and shed that I can't take with me.

I bought a lottery ticket yesterday. The drawing is tomorrow.

# Part V

# (Afterthought After the Afterthought)

# I Am a Narcissist

I am narcissistic; that's my conclusion.

I don't know if I'll ever finish this book. I think this is my third ending, but who's counting? Life persists, it moves on, and in my case, it is still confusing. I am now proceeding to my fifth part. Since completion of the previous sections, I've taken much time (*a few months*) to think long and hard about the fact that narcissists are attracted to borderline women. I have hence concluded that I am a narcissist. I don't know if my narcissistic tendencies are of the extreme variety or not. What I mean is I don't know if my narcissism is a personality disorder. Because I *am* aware of my problem, and by my own investigation and heart thinking, I think I may be a borderline narcissist (pun intended).

My now ex-wife did finally contact me. We did not talk but texted each other. Approximately three months ago, it was my birthday. I turned sixty. I don't look sixty, but I am. I don't feel sixty, but my birth certificate says I was born in 1954, so that means I really am sixty years old.

My dad would have turned eighty-one six weeks after my birthday if he would have lived. However, two months prior he began to speak with a husky voice. His doctor concluded he had stage-four lung cancer, which had spread to the rest of his organs. Two months later, he died. It was the day after my sixtieth birthday party and my son's Family Day. (Since my son was given to my first wife and me, we had celebrated the day he became our son—eight weeks after his birth—and I continue that tradition to this day. We conduct that day just like a birthday. We have a cake, ice cream, present, and I take him—and his girlfriend—out for dinner.)

My birthday was on a Tuesday. I had to work that day, till ten o'clock that night. My mom and son and his girlfriend wished me a happy birthday via phone. I now live three hours from my son and mom, so doing anything special was out of the question, especially since it was in the middle of my workweek. My coworkers did wish me happy birthday when I mentioned I was sixty years old during a meeting, which, by the way, they did not believe. Nonetheless, the next morning, there was a box of donuts on my desk when I came into work that served as a cake.

It was nice, but I was a little disappointed that such a milestone was no more special than any other day. But how could it be otherwise? I was in central Ohio, and everyone I knew was in Michigan, except for a few old work acquaintances who were almost two hours east of me at my old employer's. I wasn't depressed; I just had wished I was in Michigan so I could have celebrated with my son and family.

My present career is expanding. I am now on my way as an instructor, which had been my love for many years. Part-time teaching at church was all I could do for years, and then I was able to teach adjunct at a technical school, which eventually landed my IT chair position in eastern Ohio. As mentioned earlier, I then landed my present job, which has very good potential for growth. As most people begin winding down at age sixty, I am expanding. In fact, there are rumors I will be promoted to another state in a few months. Our school is growing, and the leaders try to promote from within. So, my profession appears to be escalating. It is very satisfying.

The Saturday after my birthday, I traveled to Michigan to celebrate my son's Family Day and to visit Mom and Dad. My son had to work Saturday, so we met at church Sunday morning. However, instead of going out for dinner, as was our usual ritual, my son told me my mom had dinner planned for us, and I needed to head there. He would meet me shortly. So, I drove to Mom and Dad's.

Speaking of my dad, he had been doing very poorly. His hoarseness was growing worse, to where it was difficult to understand him. He was still fully alert and got up and walked to the kitchen with his walker (or rode his chair into the kitchen) and appeared he still had months to live. At least, I was confident of that.

When I pulled into the driveway, I noticed many cars lining the pavement and some parked on the grass. When I got out of the car, I didn't know if I should expect a surprise holler or if they would be greeting me as another visitor for my dad. I was confident he was still doing fine, so the former is what went through my mind. I was right. Everyone yelled, "Surprise!" They had planned a surprise birthday party for me. Nobody forgot, after all.

During the midst of the party, there was reminiscing of the old days, as I was on my seventh decade now, and my cousins and friends are pushing the same. My aunts and uncles were there, as well as many cousins and friends.

The drummer from my rock band in high school was there, along with old neighbors and acquaintances. My mom and sister went all out. I believe it was, at least, partly due to my dad being on his last days. (My sister told me later that day she did not think he'd make it through the weekend, but I, being the eldest, knew better. I was sure he'd live for months yet.) The festivities lasted for hours into the late afternoon. I had two cakes; one for my sixtieth birthday and the other for my recent graduation with a master's degree. We had a good old time.

During the midst of the party, Dad came out to talk to everyone, as it was a very pretty day. He was outside for about an hour. When he went into the house, many of us followed him there and stayed with him into the evening. Two of his brothers, aged eighty-two and eighty-six, were standing beside him when my cousin began to snap a picture. Dad stopped her and insisted he stand up along with his brothers. No matter how much we all protested, he was bound and determined to stand. So, as he was doing so, two of us began to help him get up. Again, he insisted he do it alone. It wasn't a few seconds later when he began to slip and then slid down onto the floor.

My dad was a very heavy man, and whenever such things occurred, we had to call the fire department to get him up and then into a chair or the bed. This time, however, my cousin, who worked with the elderly, knew how four of us could do it. We slid a thin blanket under him, and then after forming a type of diaper, we were able to slide him back onto the chair. He then, with our help, used his walker to walk to his bed, which was in the living room a few feet away.

During this episode, my mom, crying and at her wits end said something like, "He is so bullheaded. He won't listen to a damned thing we tell him!"

Now, to most of you, this phrase was no big deal, but to me and the rest of us standing there, it was profound. First of all, my mom never gets mad when anyone other than immediate family is present. Secondly, she never uses foul language. To her, anything other than heck or darn is damnable language. Not that she considered that those who said worse were in danger of hellfire, but she just never said anything like that. The word *damned* coming from her lips will ring in my ears forever. I don't consider it terrible; in fact, I think it is somewhat cute. But, to her, Dad's bullheadedness had unknotted the last knot in her rope, and she had nothing to hang on to.

As stated earlier in this book, my mom's dad died when she was a young teenager. She had been through heartache. She saw the pains her mother went through during the years afterward. She experienced some of my pain when my wife died a number of years ago. Two of my brothers had lost wives to divorce, and most of her eight brothers and sisters were divorced. But she'd had a husband for more than sixty years. All of her kids were doing okay, and she hadn't lost any. She has many grandchildren and great-grandchildren, and all are still here.

Since that dreaded day she lost her dad, she had not lost anyone, for more than sixty years, except when her mother died. (Her mom lived to be 103 years and ten months. She lived a long and healthy life and was well prepared for it, although heartbroken for sure.) But now, *her* husband was on his deathbed. For more than sixty years they were never apart, except for when he was at work or deer hunting one week every year.

Well, there I went again—rambling. What has the above to do with my narcissistic tendencies? The fact that they gave me a sixtieth birthday party is case in point. Will my other brothers and sisters get a sixtieth party? Probably not. Did they have a surprise twenty-fifth wedding anniversary party like my family threw for me and my first wife? No, they did not. Did my other brothers and sisters get a surprise sixteenth birthday party? No, but I did.

My point is that being the oldest of seven siblings has its perks, but do these perks promote narcissistic tendencies? I don't know, and I am not trying to blame others for my problems, but I am trying to understand why I may be so consumed by my appearance of superiority and importance. I recall in the eighties when I returned to college after a ten-year break, asking God to give me a job where I could carry a briefcase. I wasn't as interested in achieving success for the money and comfort as I was in other people looking up to me, similar to the way my brothers and sisters looked up to me as we were growing up.

I had to be the best (which was simple, being the oldest), and then, while going to college, I needed to be the best. I also recall while walking between classes and buildings on campus thinking of what others thought as they saw me walking about, the big, important college man. And grades? Well, I had to get all As, not so I could land a good job when I graduated but to impress everyone with my (close to) 4.0 grade point average.

I know everyone is proud to accomplish things, but I was overly proud and needed others to tell me I was above average. When I wrote my book on church history in the midnineties, I fully expected everyone to tell me how accomplished I was with such a feat and to tell me how good the book was. It did happen to a degree, but I expected much more. When my pastor announced my book during a church service, he told the congregation how talented I was and said he was proud to have such a member in our church. He also told our bishop of my book, and the church ordered a number of copies for new pastors going through our minister's school. However, I expected more.

I expected him to help promote my book and to speak more about it and how members should tell their friends and acquaintances to purchase the book. It was not enough for him to mention it. I wanted him to expound upon the learning I had achieved and how I put it into words that lowly Christians could understand and to note that learning such things is what was important in life, and that importance was written by me!

When that did not happen, I remember complaining to my first wife how the pastor and others should be speaking more about my book. After all, it was an achievement that needed to be proclaimed to the world! She didn't say anything, but I know she considered my narcissistic tendencies to be over the top. She had told me before that I thought I knew everything. Of course, I often replied that she was wrong. I just knew most things—and yes, I was serious.

I am narcissist.

When I met my second wife, I often thought about what others would think when I walked into a room with her. When I went to church with her, I would think about how all the other guys looked at me with jealousy, realizing I had the prettiest woman on earth. I would imagine how they'd think I was the luckiest of fellows to have such a pretty woman. When we went to family gatherings, my main thoughts were, *My cousins and uncles are going to be very impressed with my pretty new wife. And, my female relatives? Why, they will be impressed too!*

When I went anywhere with her, I was in constant awareness that everyone around us had their eyes on us and were impressed with our presence. My wife was an attention getter, as she was very beautiful, and I loved the attention we drew when we walked into a room. Yes, she was my trophy.

I am narcissist.

So, did I love her because of her heart, as I did my first wife, or was it her beauty? I did ask her out because of her beauty. It was her beauty that caused me to stare at her when she walked down the hall at church. (Well, I kept my staring to a minimum. After all, I couldn't have members seeing me stare at a pretty woman in church!) Then, after I was with her for a little while, I fell in love with her voice and innocent but sexy glances at me. Then, as she told me how wonderful I was and how she had been praying to God for years to find a man such as me, I fell in love with her admiration of me. Then, as I experienced her passion, I couldn't help but fall in love with her wholeheartedly. Did I love her heart? I thought I did. However, I don't know if I really ever got to know her heart. I still don't know. I could never understand it—and I still don't.

However, I think anyone, not just a narcissist, would have fallen in love with this woman. She was beautiful in body, in speech, and in desire. What else is there? She was a Christian. She got along with my son (at least at first), although my son took a long time to accept her. (Then, of course, he rejected her when she left us the first time.) How was I not to fall in love with her? Maybe a non-narcissist would have fallen for her also, but a non-narcissist may have noticed the cues that a narcissist would not. When she said she did not want to have sex because we were not married but then asked if I wanted to go into the bedroom, may have cued a non-narcissist. When she said she was a pure and holy Christian but then stayed over till I told her she must leave before my son woke up may have clued a non-narcissist. When she said she had to clean house (before we were married) instead of coming over as usual, but then I found out she didn't need to clean house should have cued a normal person, but not me.

Maybe a non-narcissist would have married her anyway. But I am confident a non-narcissist would not have hung onto her for so many years after marriage. From our honeymoon on, it was a constant battle trying to figure her out while being bombarded with her constant false accusations.

Now, back to my original paragraph in this part five. My ex-wife and I did communicate via text after a year of her not communicating to me. A few months after our divorce, I texted her stating my dad had died. I didn't want her to come to the funeral, but I did wonder if this would break her silence. It did. She responded that she was sorry to hear about his death.

The first day at the funeral home, while my son was looking at the flowers, he noticed an arrangement from my ex-wife and her two sons. When he picked them up to throw them away, I stopped him and told him to take off the card and put the flowers on the floor in the corner. Deep down, I was glad she was beginning to communicate again, but I knew my son would never have any part of her. I still did not want to see her at the funeral home but would have liked to see her.

During the next few weeks, my ex-wife and I texted back and forth. She said things like; our marriage could have been wonderful, and it should have lasted. I said similar things. She somehow knew I had sold our house and moved. I gave her my new address when I asked her to send me the letter she told me she'd like to write stating why she left me. I never did get the letter.

Nonetheless, in her texts, she did give me bits and pieces as to why she left me. Besides the typical false accusations, she said she found e-mail files I had sent to my pastor about the troubles I was experiencing with her. These emails occurred during the interim when she had left me the first time. I had put them on a CD and inserted it with my books in my den. When we sold our house in Michigan, she found this CD among other files in the bookshelf. Instead of giving it to me, she snooped into the files (doing precisely what she claimed I was doing to her) and saw my correspondence with our pastor.

The e-mails were basically explaining my torments while she was gone the first time. I wrote to him partly for advice but mostly for relief. When I get depressed, I write. In them, I explained her weird episodes and how I wanted her to get help. My wife took them as bashings of her, and she understood them to say I did not love her. Actually, they said the very opposite. It was my pastor who replied, stating I needed to divorce her because she was not fit for me, but I replied stating I did not believe in divorce and did not want to divorce her. My wife twists things, but not intentionally. It's just her borderline personality that does not allow her to think logically. She cannot put things into perspective and consider the circumstances.

Earlier in my book, you may remember a small episode I had with her not long after we moved to Ohio. It was during our sale of the house in Michigan. That episode was apparently spurred by the emails she found when we sold our house in Michigan. She did not make me aware of these; she only read them, was eaten up by them, and did not ask me for an explanation. Our move to Ohio was doomed. Then, of course, her two sons gave her problems that caused her to pray and fast to excess, and things continued to fall apart. I spoke of all of this in the earlier parts of this book.

Well, I won't elaborate anymore, but I wonder how much of our failed marriage was due to these files that I had actually forgotten about. I didn't forget about the e-mails, but I had forgotten about the CD on the bookshelf. Either way, during our texting, which is what I am to speak about, she claimed I did not love her. Finally, I told her I loved her more than any man loved a woman, and she was wrong to leave me. Soon, however, things began to deteriorate, and she texted that I stuck a cigar up her nose and forced her to stay in a room alone for many hours, along with other accusations that I cannot recall at the moment. I was then reminded why our marriage did not last.

After a number of these false accusations I got mad at her. I replied to the text with something like, "You are a liar and an idiot! Don't bother me anymore." Before she read it, however, she sent me another text stating she should not have said those bad things about me because the Bible says we must speak well of all people. At first, I thought she may be repenting of her accusations but soon realized that was not the case. Actually, she believed that nonsense but repented of saying it. She then must have read the text I sent her, because after that, she never replied to any more of my texts. I have since erased her number from my phone and have not sent her any more. I believe I am finally over her. But, I did have hope during our texts that she may come back to me. Not now, however. So, in truth, I am now 98 percent over her. But I know, if she showed up at my door, I would take her back. Am I a narcissist, a Christian, or just an idiot?

My answer is; I am all of the above. So, I sit in my apartment, wishing things were different.

**The End (For Sure)**

# Notes

## (Endnotes)

1. Throughout the Bible, especially Revelation (tongue-in-cheek).
2. Hebrews (He Brews) in New Testament (tongue-in-cheek again).
3. "Professing themselves to be wise they became fools." (Romans 1:22 KJV)
4. Speaking of changes in marriage, I'm holding in my hand an issue of Bloomberg Businessweek from September 2013 issue. An article titled, "Leaving Him Behind to Get Ahead" by Charles Kenny almost glorifies divorce. He says that now women can leave their husbands fairly easily. This allows them to leave an unhappy or unhealthy marriage in pursuit of better things. As countries allow easy divorce, women advance in society. I think this may be true, but it causes undue torment to her husband and to the children. Kenny agrees that children may be hurt, but to hell with the husbands. My lowly opinion is that today's society has a low opinion of other people and too high of an opinion of ourselves. The Golden Rule means nothing today.
5. Lauren Hansen. "9 Negative Effects Divorce reportedly Has on Children," The Week, March 28, 2013, Retrieved April 2, 2013, from http://theweek.com/article/index/242059/9-negative-effects-divorce-reportedly-has-on-children
6. The phrase "making the dash count" refers to the dash on a person's tombstone. Date of birth, dash, date of death.

7. On one of his TV sermons. I cannot find the episode, nor the date.
8. W.R. Owens, edit., *The Pilgrim's Progress of John Bunyan* (Oxford: Oxford World's Classics, 2003.

   I am speaking of his character named Help, found in part one.
9. Lee Brice, vocal performance of "I Drive Your Truck," by Jessi Alexander, Connie Harrington, and Jimmy Yeary, released December 3, 2012, Curb. The song is about a brother who was killed in action but was inspired by a father who lost his son in Afghanistan.
10. Shadowlands, directed by Richard Attenborough (1993; Price Entertainment).
11. Thomas Paine, Common Sense, 1776. Accessed 2013. http://www.ushistory.org/paine/commonsense/
12. Confucius. (~551–479BC). The Negative Golden Rule (sometimes called The Silver Rule because it is the negative version) is in his Analects.
13. My Big Fat Greek Wedding, directed by Joel Zwick (2002; Gold Circle Films). Accessed 2013. http://www.fanpop.com/clubs/my-big-fat-greek-wedding/articles/8854/title/big-fat-greek-wedding-quotes
14. Dr. Sharon Lloyd, PhD in Philosophy of Counseling. Redeemer Fellowship Church. (http://e-christiancounsel.com/COUNSELING.html)
15. Proverbs 23:20–21, 28:7, 23:2; Deuteronomy 21:20; 2 Peter 1:5–7; 2 Timothy 3:1–9; 2 Corinthians 10:5
16. Proverbs 23:3, 20–21, 28:7; Deuteronomy 21:20; 2 Peter 1:5–7; 2 Timothy 3:1–9; 2 Corinthians 10:5
17. See the following websites: http://www.illinoissmokersrights.com/tobacco_timeline.html, http://archive.tobacco.org/resources/history/Tobacco_History.html, or http://www.tobacco.org/resources/history/Tobacco_History.html
18. The phrase "Moderation in all things" comes from Aristotle's Doctrine of the Mean (Nicomachean Ethics). Finding the mean, or middle ground, between excess and deficiency.

19. David Ross, trans., *Nicomachean Ethics of Aristotle* (New York: Oxford University Press, 1925)
20. PBS, Detroit Public TV. Prohibition. Roots of Prohibition. 2011. Accessed 2013. http://www.pbs.org/kenburns/prohibition/roots-of-prohibition/
21. History.com. "18th and 21st Amendments." (2014) http://www.history.com/topics/18th-and-21st-amendments & http://history1900s.about.com/od/1920s/p/prohibition.htm
22. "Temperance Movement" on the website for Encyclopaedia Britannica, http://www.britannica.com/EBchecked/topic/586530/temperance-movement. Also, for a list of prohibition countries see http://en.wikipedia.org/wiki/List_of_countries_with_alcohol_prohibition. Note, however, only a few non-Muslim countries. Islam does not believe in drinking alcohol.
23. Tongue in cheek. My dad did make wine. Jesus's miracle of wine was the finest, however. John 2:1–11.
24. Philip Schaff, *History of the Christian Church, Volume IV* (Grand Rapids: WM. B. Eerdmans Publishing Company, 1910)
25. Leviticus 11:7.
26. See references above on prohibition and temperance movement. History is basically silent as to Christians not drinking wine except for a few fringe groups. Jews and Chistians, for 1900 years, do not deny wine to the masses of Christians. I cannot find one instance anywhere, where a Jew of Jesus' day, or a Christian theologian denied the use of wine, prior to the 19th century.
27. Proverbs 20:1 describes drinking in excess, not drinking moderately. This was the understanding of virtually all of the Church until the Temperance movement in the nineteenth century.
28. Matthew 5:32 speaks of divorce, which only makes sense if the person can remarry. This fornication is physical adultery, not the adultery in the heart spoken of earlier in the chapter.
29. I Corinthians 7.

30. Walter I. Brandt, trans., *The Estate of Marriage by Martin Luther,* 'Luther's Works,' Vol. 45. Retrieved from http://www.teleiosministries.com/martin-luther-on-marriage-divorce.html
31. See endnote iv that speaks on the Newsweek article.
32. PDF of the book in http://www.ccel.org/ccel/bunyan/pilgrim.pdf
33. I cannot reveal the title of this church history book as I am the author. The book you are now reading is under my pen name. My history book is under my real name. Therefore the reason for not rendoring my church history book details.
34. 1 Corinthians 14:23.
35. Luke 6:23; Acts 3:1–11.
36. Matthew 5:28.
37. Matthew 5:21–26.
38. Genesis 24:67.
39. While proofing my book, I am reminded of the time my present (now ex) wife became boiling mad at me because she thought I wanted to have sex with this nephew's sister—my niece—when they stayed at our house during the funeral of my nieces' and my son's grandmother.
40. Suzanne Somers, The *Sexy Years: Discover the Hormone Connection: The Secret to Fabulous Sex, Great Health, and Vitality, for Women and Men* (New York: Harmony Publishers, 2005).
41. Jerold J. Kreisman and Hal Straus, *I Hate You—Don't Leave Me.* (New York: Avon Books, 1989).
42. I had purchased this vacant lot that was adjacent to my house over 25 years ago. When I sold the house in Michigan, I told him I'd give it to him to build on when he got married later in life. However, I now needed the money I would receive in its sale to pay for his college dorm, etc. It is ironic, when my second wife left me the final time, she took out a $60k loan in my name and left. I am now left to pay that loan back, of which is twice the lot's worth. The story is too long to tell here.
43. Reference to the City of Destruction. W.R. Owens, edit., *The Pilgrim's Progress of John Bunyan*
44. Jerold J. Kreisman and Hal Straus, *I Hate You—Don't Leave Me.*

45. "Facing the Facts. How a Borderline Personality Disorder Love Relationship Evolves," Roger Melton, M.A. Accessed 2014, http://bpdfamily.com/bpdresources/nk_a101.htm
46. "Facing the Facts. How a Borderline Personality Disorder Love Relationship Evolves,"
47. "Facing the Facts. How a Borderline Personality Disorder Love Relationship Evolves,"
48. "Facing the Facts. How a Borderline Personality Disorder Love Relationship Evolves,"
49. Gina Piccalo, "Sex on the Edge." The Daily Beast. Posted June 21, 2010. Accessed 2014. http://www.thedailybeast.com/articles/2010/06/21/borderline-personality-disorder-and-sex.html.
50. Gina Piccalo, "Sex on the Edge."
51. Gina Piccalo, "Sex on the Edge."
52. Paul T. Mason and Randi Kreger, *Stop Walking on Eggshells: Taking Your Life Back When Someone You Care about Has Borderline Personality Disorder* (Oakland, CA.: New Harbinger Publications, 1998).
53. Paul T. Mason and Randi Kreger, *Stop Walking on Eggshells: Taking Your Life Back When Someone You Care about Has Borderline Personality Disorder*
54. Paul T. Mason and Randi Kreger, *Stop Walking on Eggshells: Taking Your Life Back When Someone You Care about Has Borderline Personality Disorder*
55. Anna North, "Borderline Personality Disorder Is Damn Sexy! Right?" Jezebel. Posted on June 22, 2010. Accessed 2014. http://jezebel.com/5569674/introducing-the-boarderline-personality-sexy-fenne-fatale.
56. Robert O. Friedel, *Borderline Personality Disorder Demystified: An Essential Guide for Understanding and Living with BPD* (Philadelphia: Da Capo Press Lifelong Books, 2004).
57. Rachel Reiland, *Get Me Out of Here: My Recovery from Borderline Personality Disorder* (Center City, MN: Eggshells Press, 2002).
58. Jerold J. Kreisman and Hal Straus, *I Hate You—Don't Leave Me.*

59. Fatal Attraction, directed by Adrian Lyne (1987; Paramount Pictures).
60. Gerald P. Koocher, John C. Norcorss, and Beverly A. Greene, eds., *Psychologists' Desk Reference* (Oxford: Oxford University Press, 2013).
61. Who's Afraid of Virginia Woolf? directed by Mike Nichols (1966; Warner Bros.).
62. Mrs. Parker and the Vicious Circle, directed by Alan Rudolph (1994; Fine Line Features).